Feb 2

The Best of

THREE MINUTES
A DAY

Other Christopher Books in Print

The Best of

Three Minutes
A Day

Volumes 1 - 5

25th volume in a series containing inspirational stories and reflections for each day of the year.

Father James Keller, M.M.

Founder, The Christophers

With an Introduction by
Father John Catoir

Director, The Christophers

Compiled and edited by
Joseph R. Thomas
and Margaret O'Connell

THE CHRISTOPHERS, 12 East 48th St., New York, NY 10017

Know that the Lord is God!
It is He that made us and we are His;
we are His people,
and the sheep of His pasture.
Enter His gates with thanksgiving,
and His courts with praise!
Give thanks to Him, bless His name!
For the Lord is good;
His steadfast love endures for ever . . .

Psalm 100:3-5

Introduction

From time to time I have occasion to delve into early volumes in our Three Minutes a Day series of books. Whenever I do I am struck by the relevancy of so much of the material, even 40 years after initial publication.

Many of those early books were best-sellers in the popular market. It is easy to understand why. Father James Keller, founder of The Christophers and the author of all those early works, was nothing if not meticulous in his writing.

We've talked about that here in the office, where we still have some people recruited for The Christophers by Father Keller. I don't know who first brought the subject up, but it seemed like a natural: why not publish an anthology of some of the very best pieces from those early Three Minutes a Day books.

And so you hold in your hands the first such anthology, "The Best of Three Minutes a Day, Volumes 1 through 5." Obviously there will be other anthologies if interest in this initial volume proves to be as strong as we expect.

People still write to us and tell us about coming across a particular piece in a book bought at a garage sale, or found in an attic. Sifting through the early volumes has been a monumental task for our editors, Joseph R. Thomas and Margaret O'Connell. They were given free rein with these stipulations:

▪ Choose only the very best.

▪ Choose pieces that have contemporary application.

▪ Retain the flavor of Father Keller's writing by making only those revisions that are absolutely necessary.

What follows then is Father Keller's work. It testifies to his wisdom and his foresight. We present it secure in the knowledge that students of spirituality cite Father Keller as one of the principal influences on American spiritual life because of his understanding of the concept of individual mission: the notion that all are called to a Gospel life by God and are to fulfill that mission in their own family, work and community environment.

Father John Catoir

Gratitude, Link to Love

A few days after Christmas a six-year-old boy was trudging down San Francisco's crowded Pine St., dragging a glistening new wagon with a tiny baby passenger — a statue of the Christ Child from the crib of the neighborhood church. Horrified, the boy's mother ran down the street and reprimanded him sharply.

"But, Mother," the boy protested, wide-eyed, "I promised the Baby Jesus that if He gave me a wagon for Christmas, He would have the first ride in it."

The first day of the New Year is a most appropriate time to express our thanks to God for the blessings He has showered on all of us. Show Him your appreciation in any manner you wish — but do show Him.

One way would be to reach beyond your own little group to bring Christ's love to a lonely or sick person.

By this shall all know that you are My disciples if you have love for one another. (Jn. 13:35)

Jesus, help us express our gratitude to You in loving service to our sisters and brothers.

No Shortcut

A prominent businessman who was enrolling his son in a well-known university shook his head dubiously when he began to examine the institution's catalogue of studies.

"Does my son have to take all these courses?" he asked the dean. "Can't you make it shorter? He wants to get out quickly."

"Certainly he can take a shorter course," replied the dean. "But it all depends on what he wants to make of himself. When God wants to make an oak He takes 20 years, but He only takes two months to make a squash."

Shortcuts attract all of us. And of course we are free to take the easy way out. But just as oaks do not grow overnight, neither do the mind and character.

He that is patient, is governed with much wisdom: but he that is impatient, exalts his folly. (Pr. 14:29)

Pray for the patience to develop the best God has put in you!

Don't Miss the Obvious

There is an ancient tale about a king who wanted to pick the wisest man among his subjects to be his prime minister. When the search finally narrowed down to just three men, he decided to put them to the supreme test.

Accordingly, he placed them together in a room in his palace, and on the room door he had installed a lock which was the last word in mechanical ingenuity. The candidates were informed that whoever was able to open the door first would be appointed to the post of honor.

The three men immediately set themselves to the task. Two of them began at once to work out complicated mathematical formulas to discover the proper lock combination.

The third man, however, just sat down in his chair, lost in thought. Finally, without bothering to put pen to paper, he got up, walked to the door, and turned the handle. And the door opened to his touch. It had been unlocked all the time!

Ask, and it shall be given you; seek and you shall find; knock and it shall be opened to you. (Mt. 7:7)

Pray that you will use the means that Christ Himself gives you to reach your eternal goal.

A Soft Answer . . .

One day, despite warnings, Donald Carey, a 13-year-old boy, climbed over a four-foot fence and ventured too far into an area reserved for two polar bears at the Forest Park Zoo in St. Louis. He narrowly escaped with his life.

The two bears, "Snowball" and "Frisky" — favorites at the zoo for years — suddenly grabbed Donald by the legs, pulled him into the pit, and began to bite and pummel him.

He was rescued only when attendants, attracted by the screams of children outside the fence, rushed to the scene, drove off the bears, and pulled him free. Later, the director of the zoo said that the only reason the boy escaped with his life, even though he's been mauled by the huge animals for almost 15 minutes, was because "he did not try to fight the bears."

Make friends quickly with your accuser. (Mt. 5:25)

God, teach me how to disagree without being disagreeable!

It Takes Courage

A man who took great pride in his lawn found himself with a large crop of dandelions. After trying every method he knew to get rid of them, he wrote the Department of Agriculture. He enumerated all the things he had tried, and closed his letter with the question: "What shall I do now?"

In due course came the reply, "We suggest you learn to love them."

The Christopher approach always stresses positive action in remedying a seemingly hopeless situation. If one method fails, try another.

"The difficult we do right away . . . The impossible takes a little longer."

Be watchful, stand firm in your faith, be courageous, be strong. Let all that you do be done in love. (1 Cor. 16:13)

Lord, give me the courage to change what can be changed; the patience to bear what cannot be changed; the wisdom to tell the one from the other.

The Three Wise Men

Today used to be called Little Christmas. The Gospel narrative, the second chapter of St. Matthew, tells in brief but forceful detail how the three Kings, Magi, or Wise Men, as they are called, came from afar to pay tribute to the Infant Savior.

In their faith, hope and charity there is an inspirational lesson for all:

They were honest and straightforward. Despite the suspicions of Herod, they frankly stated their quest and their allegiance: "Where is He who has been born king of the Jews? For we have seen His star in the East, and have come to worship Him." (Mt. 2:2)

They were confronted with many difficulties. After a long and dangerous journey, guided only by a lone star, they were met with trickery on the part of Herod, who said to them: "Go and search diligently for the Child, and when you have found Him bring me word, that I too may come and worship Him." (Mt. 2:8)

They were happy in their search for Christ: "They rejoiced exceedingly with great joy." (Mt. 2:10)

And going into the house they saw the Child with Mary His Mother, and they fell down and worshiped Him. Then, opening their treasures, they offered Him gifts, gold and frankincense and myrrh. (Mt. 2:11)

God give us the grace to be Christ-bearers in all circumstances — no matter what the cost.

Fair Exchange

At a crowded intersection while waiting for the light to change, a car stalled, holding up a line of other vehicles. Obviously flustered, the man who was driving the car hurriedly got out and lifted the hood to investigate. As he did, the driver of the car behind began honking his horn.

The noise kept on without letup until the driver of the stalled car straightened up and spoke to the impatient motorist behind him.

"If you'll fix my car," he said calmly, "I'll be glad to keep blowing your horn for you."

In our own impatience we sometimes think that mere noises will make a bad situation right itself. We think that if we shout loud enough everyone will be bound to hear and lend a hand.

Actually, impatience over trivial annoyances often makes matters worse. On the other hand, realistic appraisal of the situation and considered, thoughtful action are the best guarantee of quick, profitable results.

A soft answer turns away wrath but a harsh word stirs up anger. (Prov. 15:1)

Lord, help me to be as calm and patient with others as You are with me.

The Motive Counts

At an elaborate coming-out party the wealthy matron responsible for it beamed in triumph. Her months of careful preparation and the money she'd spent on it were being well rewarded.

Guest after guest, fortified with an abundance of champagne, rushed up to her and gushed, "This is the party of parties!" or "I've never seen anything like it before!"

The person for whom the affair was actually given, the matron's daughter, was little more than a figurehead in all the festivities.

She regretfully remarked to a friend: "My mother didn't give that party for me. She gave it for herself. I was only the excuse!"

All of us are in constant danger of getting our motives mixed. Even the most charitable of works can be used as an "excuse" to further one's personal ambitions. And many use a good cause for their private advantage. Their object is not to do good for others, but to do well for themselves.

Each tree is known by its own fruit. (Lk. 6:44)

May we perform all our good works not for self-aggrandizement, but for the benefit of others.

No Easy Way

A young man, just beginning the study of musical composition, once went to Mozart to ask him the formula for developing the theme of a symphony. Mozart suggested that a symphony was rather an ambitious project for a beginner: perhaps the young man might better try his hand at something simpler first.

"But you were writing symphonies when you were my age," the student protested.

"Yes," the famous composer answered. "But I didn't have to ask how."

The beginner in any field is often impatient, eager for quick results. Yet the time spent in preparing a firm groundwork is not time wasted.

Particularly is this true of those who would help others for the love of God. For most of us there is no quick, easy, or lazy way. It is a question of daily plodding, often in the face of discouragement, misunderstanding, and obstacles. Perseverance is the test of our sincerity.

Be imitators of those who through faith and long suffering inherit the promises. (Heb. 6:12)

Lord give us the grace to make haste — slowly.

Don't Let Changes Startle You

"Hey, you've got elephants in your yard!" was the report that greeted an Oregon man upon opening his front door.

The man hurried out to take a look. Sure enough, there he saw, not one elephant, but three!

The amazed man learned afterwards that a collision had tipped over a circus truck nearby and spilled the animals to unexpected freedom.

Most of us don't need an invasion of elephants to be convinced that we are living in a lightning-fast world that is filled with unexpected developments.

Technical and social changes are bringing many benefits but also posing new challenges. As a follower of Christ you must do more than scratch your head at the forces of change.

Do your part by keeping abreast of international news and making the world's crises the object of your prayers. And persuade your friends to do the same.

Let us not sleep, as others do, but let us keep awake and be sober. (1 Th. 5:6)

Grant me grace, Father, to confront the continuing rapid changes of life and not evade my duty.

Limitless Horizons

Some time ago I took a trip. During the journey I turned to the man next to me and asked: "Can you tell me the name of the next station?"

"Sorry, I can't," the stranger replied. "I've been riding this line for 15 years and I only know two stops: where I get on and where I get off."

There are many people who limit their horizons as did this traveler. They concern themselves with saving their own souls — which is of first importance — but fail to concern themselves with trying to help save the souls of others. They think merely in terms of their origin and destiny. They overlook their fellow human beings who are searching for God.

A bearer of Christ not only knows where he/she comes from and where he/she is going. A Christ-bearer helps others find their way to God, too.

What you hear whispered, proclaim upon the housetops. (Mt. 10:27)

Pray that you may extend your vision beyond your immediate circle.

The Little Extra Called Kindness

A little town with a big heart was the way one newspaper account described Andrews, N.C. A couple who had an automobile accident there found this out through personal experience.

A lumberman and his wife from Memphis crashed near Andrews when their car missed a curve. The wife was critically injured but the husband, though hurt, was not hospitalized.

Visitors poured into the hospital offering to help the stranded people. Invitations came from all sides for the husband to stay in local homes. While the family car was being fixed, several townspeople offered him the use of their cars.

When the injured woman was able to travel, but only by ambulance, the hospital arranged for the ambulance driver to take them on the 440-mile trip at a remarkably low price.

Even in the impersonal atmosphere of modern life, you can, in the spirit of Christ, add your personal touch to lighten the burden of those in need. Take that extra step today to leave things better than you found them.

Let brotherly love continue. Do not neglect to show hospitality to strangers, for thereby some have entertained angels unawares. (Heb. 13:1)

Make me ever mindful, O Lord, that my slightest kindness is pleasing to You.

The Best Treatment

An eminent baby specialist had a standard treatment for frail newborn infants who failed to gain weight and thrive: "This baby is to be loved very three hours."

Not only do newborn babies need affection. Doctors agree that many of our physical ills result from a feeling of insecurity or loneliness, of not being wanted.

While this is true of our physical illnesses, how much more is it true of our spiritual illnesses.

Love of neighbor remains the best remedy for all illnesses — both for our neighbor and for ourselves.

Let love be genuine . . . love one another . . . outdo one another in showing honor. (Rom. 12:9,10)

Jesus, teach me to love especially Your least children with the same love with which You love me.

Worry Solves Little

It was well past midnight and still the old man could not sleep. "It's evil, hopelessly evil — this world of ours," he thought. "It's wicked and doomed."

Then, suddenly, it seemed to him that he heard a voice speaking in the darkness. It was, he felt, the voice of an angel.

"Go to sleep, old man," it seemed to say; "I'll sit up the rest of the night."

Anxiety never baked a cake, built a bridge, won a battle, or solved a problem. Important as we are, we really render ourselves less useful — and less important — if we let worry stall our action.

The best thing we can do is work on the opportunities God gives us and leave the production of the "show" to the Divine Director.

Why are you fearful, O you of little faith? (Mt. 8:26)

O my God, I put my worries in Your Hands.

One Small Light

Some time ago I had occasion to visit the Metropolitan Opera House in New York. It was late at night, after the performance, and all the employees except the assistant manager had gone home. He asked me to wait until he could turn on the main lights and went down the aisle and mounted the stage alone.

As I waited, scarcely able to see the outline of his figure in the darkness, there was the sound of a match striking wood, then a tiny sliver of light appeared. Yet small as it was, it was greater than all the blackness around it.

After that it was but the work of a moment to multiply its minute glow thousands of times and dispel the shadows which still remained. With the click of a switch, clusters of electric lights flooded the opera house, and the darkness was gone.

The least person, no matter how insignificant he may feel, who is interested in bringing the light of Christ's truth to the whole world, is a pinpoint of light in the darkness, greater than all the encircling gloom. Darkness disappears in the same proportion as light is added. It is as simple as that.

> **You are the light of the world . . . Let your light so shine before men, that they may see your good works and give glory to your Father. (Mt. 5:14,16)**

> *Lord, strengthen me to do my part in bearing Your light to all humankind.*

Perseverance Pays Off

In one of the decisive battles of World War I disastrous reports poured into the headquarters of Marshal Foch, the commander of the Allied forces.

The great general, faced with reverses that would have overwhelmed most of us, never lost heart. When things were at their worst, he drafted his famous order which is now in all textbooks of military strategy:

"My center is giving way, my right is pushed back, my left is wavering. The situation is excellent. I shall attack!"

The success that followed the Allied attack broke the spine of the armies of the Central Powers.

There is an old and true saying that the battle is won by the force which stays in the field for the last 15 minutes. A boxer becomes a champion by staying in the ring right up to the last bell. The surgeon who doesn't lose his nerve, but fights beyond hope, is the one who saves the "hopeless" cases.

He who endures to the end, will be saved. (Mt. 24:13)

Jesus, help me to persevere in the face of the most discouraging obstacles.

The Rain Always Stops

As William Dean Howells and Mark Twain were coming out of church one morning it commenced to rain heavily.

"Do you think it will ever stop?" asked Howells.

"It always has," answered Twain.

Unpleasant situations have a way of appearing eternal, but we can always bear in mind that nothing in this world is permanent. There is no evil that we cannot attack by faith, by good works, and by our prayers.

In this sense, a "healthy optimism" seems the natural point of view for all believers in God's goodness.

Rejoice in the Lord, always. (Phil. 4:4)

We pray that we may never lose faith in Your mercy, Lord.

Satan's Most Valuable Tool

One day, as fiction has it, the Devil decided to go out of business. His tools, therefore, being for sale, were put on display; and Malice, Jealousy, and Pride were soon recognized by most of his prospective customers.

There was one worn, tiny, wedge-shaped tool bearing the highest price, however, which seemed difficult to identify.

"What is that?" someone asked. "I can't quite place it."

"Oh, that!" Satan answered. "That is Discouragement. It is my most valuable tool. With it I can open many hearts, since so few people know that it belongs to me."

But discouragement does belong to Satan. And one of the most effective protections against discouragement is the comforting (and true) conviction that Christ is ever with us. We are His. He loves us.

It is I; have no fear. (Mt. 14:27)

Holy Spirit, obtain for us that courage which only You can.

Meaning of the Word

The word Christopher is derived from the Greek *Christophoros*, which means "Christ-bearer." With the aim of restoring to all phases of life, public and private, divine truth and human integrity, the Christopher goes into the market place, into a job of his own choosing, without fanfare or flagwaving.

He is not out to do anything sensational. His task is to insist on truth where others are insisting on falsehood. Where there is hate, he brings in love; where there is darkness, he carries light.

The Christopher emphasizes the normal rather than the abnormal. Nothing remarkable may ever be required of him beyond a generous spirit of daring.

He expects to do the usual, not the unusual; the ordinary, not the extraordinary. He knows that while the steady fulfillment of duty often involves monotony and drudgery, yet his continuing sacrifice is ever lightened by a driving purpose.

The most trivial and tiresome task achieves significance when done for Christ.

My yoke is sweet and My burden light. (Mt. 11:30)

Lord, help me to accomplish great things for You by doing the little things at hand.

She Got Double Instead of Nothing

A billfold lying on a San Francisco sidewalk attracted the attention of a 21-year-old college student. She discovered $25 in cash in it, together with the owner's name and address.

Without delay she returned it to the owner — a doctor in Oakland, Cal.

A few days later a card reached the student from the doctor.

"Many thanks for your honesty," it read. "And may God bless you."

Enclosed was a money order for $50.

While there may be little chance of your experiencing such a happy ending, this is no reason for being less zealous to see that honesty prevails in every field you can influence.

Keep on the lookout for the little things and the big things usually fall into line. If you can do that extra bit of work your job requires and show a tireless devotion to the securing of the God-given rights for others, you will have a reward that is more than financial.

Let us then cast off the works of darkness and put on the armor of light; let us conduct ourselves becomingly as in the day. (Rom. 13:12)

Keep me ever aware, O Holy Spirit, of each day's opportunities to offer You the service of a devotion to justice.

Recognition Is Not Everything

Paul Cezanne never suspected that he would some day be considered "the father of modern painting." Because of his great love for his work, he never thought of recognition. He struggled for 35 years, living in oblivion at Aix, France, giving away masterpieces to indifferent neighbors.

Then one day a discerning Paris dealer happened upon his canvases and, gathering several of them, presented the first Cezanne exhibit. The greats of the art world were stunned: here, indeed, was a master!

Cezanne himself was no less astonished. Arriving at the gallery on the arm of his son, he gazed wonderingly at his paintings, and tears came to his eyes.

"Look," he whispered. "They've framed them!"

Had it been Cezanne's chief aim to be hailed as a great artist, he might never have achieved much of anything. He achieved greatness simply by trying to make use of the artistic talents God had given him, in the very best way he knew how.

Am I now seeking the favor of men, or of God? . . . If I were still pleasing men, I should not be a servant of Christ. (Gal. 1:10)

Christ, may we seek only to please You with our lives.

Small Compromises, Trivial Evasions

Recently a large group of "problem" children were given the assignment of writing essays on the difficulties they had with their parents.

The papers they turned in were misspelled but lively, listing a number of rather expectable faults. But oddly enough the quality most children felt their parents lacked was *truthfulness*.

None of us, of course, likes to think of himself as a liar. In important things we make it a point to be scrupulously honest. But if we examine our daily lives closely we may find dozens of examples of small compromises, trivial evasions.

These seemingly unimportant deceits can all too easily become a part of the fabric of our existence and influence our relationships with others.

In nowise speak against the truth, but be ashamed of the lie. (Ecc. 4:30)

O God of truth, grant me that delicate sense of honesty which will help me to avoid all deceit.

Millions Have — So Can You!

As the harassed driver approaches an extremely narrow pass on a tortuous road in the Rocky Mountains, he is confronted by the following reassuring sign:

"Oh, yes, you can. Millions have."

Sometimes we cannot help but think: "Nobody has ever been as badly off as I am now."

When we brood over them, our ills enlarge themselves until they obscure our entire horizon. Yet, if we think of some of the things others have had to suffer, and especially if we remember the unfailing grace of God, our troubles become easier to bear.

We realize that it is a part of our human situation to undergo pain, and the eternal reward comes more clearly to mind.

I will show him how much he must suffer for the sake of my name. (Acts 9:16)

Lord, help me to bear ills bravely for Your name's sake.

Teenager Saves Eight

No sooner did 15-year-old Rejean Robarge smell smoke than he leapt from his second story farmhouse window in Lowell, Vt.

His parents were away for a while and it was his job to save his eight younger brothers and sisters. Running to the barn, he grabbed a ladder and slammed it against the side of the building.

He scurried up the ladder and led the younger ones out, one by one, barefoot and in their nightclothes, to the snow-covered ground. A nose count revealed that one small boy was still missing.

The teenager dashed once more into the now flaming structure and snatched the youngster from a smoke-filled downstairs room. He then piled the family on a tractor and drove them a mile to a neighbor's house.

Teenagers are capable of such cool heroism when properly motivated. Bring out the God-given potential in young people by encouraging their best efforts, restraining them with tact, and opening their eyes to a life's work in the vital fields that shape world trends.

Deal courageously, and may the Lord be with the upright! (2 Chr. 19:11)

Make me Your instrument, O Holy Spirit, in bringing out the power waiting to be tapped in young people.

Light for Our Darkness

Sir William Blackstone, the great English jurist, writing in his "Commentaries on the Laws of England" in 1769, was most explicit in emphasizing the weakness of man's nature. As he observed:

". . . if our reason were always, as in our first ancestor before his transgression, clear and perfect, unruffled by passions, unclouded by prejudice, unimpaired by disease or intemperance, the task would be pleasant and easy; we should need no other guide but this. But every man now finds the contrary in his own experience; that his reason is corrupt, and his understanding full of ignorance and error."

At the same time Blackstone pointed out how God is constantly helping us:

"This has given manifold occasion for the benign interposition of divine Providence, which, in compassion to the frailty, the imperfection, and the blindness of human reason, hath been pleased at sundry times and in divers manners, to discover and enforce its laws by an immediate and direct revelation. The doctrines thus delivered we call the revealed or divine law . . ."

Without Me, you can do nothing. (Jn. 15:5)

To my feeble efforts add Your strength and power, O God.

The Greatest Empire

Napoleon, in his lonely exile on St. Helena, had much time for thought. And some of his reflections were highly interesting. This one, for instance:

"Alexander, Caesar, Charlemagne, and I founded great empires. But upon what did the creation of our genius depend? Upon force. Jesus alone founded His empire upon love, and to this very day millions would die for Him."

Christ taught in a new way founded on love. The world had never before heard of this love. And even now, nineteen centuries later, more than half the world is still ignorant of His love.

Often Jesus seems to lose, but in reality He always wins — by love.

A new commandment I give to you: that you love one another, as I have loved you. (Jn. 13:34)

O God, I want to love You as You have loved me.

Accident Victim Was His Son

An emergency call brought an ambulance screaming through Long Beach, Cal., to the scene of an accident. The driver knew the neighborhood well. It was where he lived.

Braking his vehicle to a halt, he jumped out to administer first aid to an injured six-year-old boy. The driver of the accident car had covered the lad's face with his jacket, but the youngster's unruly blond hair was strikingly visible.

"My God," gasped the ambulance driver as he took a closer look. "It's my own son."

Hardly ever does it happen that the person we help unawares turns out to be a close relative. But, in another way, everyone to whom we extend a hand of kindness is our close relative. If you want to be a true child of your heavenly Father, do all you can for His other children.

Have we not all one father? Has not one God created us? Why then are we faithless to one another, profaning the covenant? (Mal. 2:10)

Let me see You, O Father, in all the members of the human family who look to me for assistance.

No Second Edition

In the early 19th century the poet John Clare wrote ironically: "If life had a second edition, how I would correct the proofs!"

All of us have but one "turn at bat" here on earth to prepare for eternity. Yet, while on earth we can learn from our past mistakes, can avoid making them in the future, and can fill our lives with concern for the spiritual and material welfare of others as well as ourselves.

Those who strive to carry Christ into the dust and heat of the marketplace will have with them the Light which will illumine the road to eternal salvation.

Mistakes they may make, but with Him to guide them, they will never wander very far from His Peace and Truth.

Now indeed you have sorrow; but I will see you again, and your heart shall rejoice; and your joy no one shall take from you. (Jn. 16:22)

Lord, be my help, my joy and my strength.

A Sure Way to Fail

Newsweek magazine in a brief article under the heading, "The Hard Road to Ruin," once listed a number of sure-fire ways to ruin a business career and become an outstanding failure. Among these were the following:

■ If a subordinate makes a mistake, let him/her have both barrels, preferably in front of others.

■ Never accept responsibility for a decision if you can possibly avoid it.

■ Develop your ability to pass the buck — take private lessons at night if need be.

■ Be so impatient for advancement that you fail to learn what your present job has to teach.

■ The same means of achieving failure in a business career can be paralleled in many other walks of life. An unwillingness to accept personal responsibility and to disagree without becoming disagreeable are certain means of antagonizing others.

Similarly, a reluctance to learn how to handle a given situation invariably does untold damage.

Have nothing to do with stupid, senseless controversies . . . (do) not be quarrelsome but kindly to every one . . . forbearing . . . with gentleness. (2 Tim. 2:23-25)

Lord, teach me never to shirk responsibility or put another down in my quest for success.

Sympathy Isn't Enough

On a mountain trail in the Andes a traveler met a farmer riding on a mule, while his wife walked along behind him.

"Why isn't your wife riding?" the traveler asked the farmer.

"Because," the farmer replied, "she has no mule."

It is even possible, when you come to think of it, that the farmer felt sorry for his wife. He may have thought to himself; "Too bad my wife has to walk. Now if only she had a mule! . . ."

How often we do this. How often we fail to help those in need, out of the abundance of the things we possess, yet feel sorry for them. We express sympathy and do nothing. And all the while there lies at hand the means whereby we could relieve their burden.

As long as you did it not to one of the least of these you did it not to Me. (Mt. 25:45)

Grant us, O Lord, to know not only what we ought to do, but the way in which we can do it.

Hamburger With Something Extra

A hamburger seasoned with $1,000 in bills was handed to a man in a Los Angeles restaurant.

Ten minutes later the honest buyer returned and confronted the waitress with the treasure she had inadvertently given away.

She blanched as she looked at the money. It was the day's receipts, which she had left for a moment on the counter in a paper bag and had included in his take-out order.

"You don't want me to eat this, do you?" he asked playfully.

Indeed she did not. Despite her entreaties, the man would not even accept a cup of coffee.

"Money is a good servant," runs an old proverb, "but a bad master." This is especially true when it belongs to somebody else.

Without denying the value of material possessions, try always to keep them subject to the laws of God, the welfare of your neighbor and your own spiritual development. Then they will be truly good servants.

I have no silver and gold, but I give you what I have. (Acts 3:6)

Never let a yearning for material treasures betray me, Lord, into upsetting the order You have established.

the first two commandments,
tablets should be the former
Do you remember them?
your God

A Way of Living

A missioner once showed one of his parishioners the Ten Commandments. "Why, they are very reasonable," she said, "I don't see how anyone can very well get on without them."

The Ten Commandments, God's program for right relationships, should be the foundation of our way of life.

Do you remember them?

■ I am the Lord your God; you shall not have strange gods before Me.

■ You shall not take the name of the Lord your God in vain.

■ Remember to keep holy the Sabbath day.

■ Honor your father and your mother.

■ You shall not kill.

■ You shall not commit adultery.

■ You shall not steal.

■ You shall not bear false witness against your neighbor.

■ You shall not covet your neighbor's wife.

■ You shall not covet your neighbor's goods.

Hear the commandments of life, O Israel; give ear and learn . . . where there is wisdom, where there is strength, where there is understanding. (Bar. 3:9,14)

Divine Lawgiver, help us order our relationships according to Your commandments.

No Automatic Champion

When Babe Didrickson Zaharias, often called the "athletic phenomenon of all time," won the British woman's golf championship, people said of her what they had said many times before: "Oh, she's an automatic champion, a natural athlete." But the facts tell a different story.

"When Babe started golfing in earnest . . ." an article stated, "she hit as many as 1,000 balls in one afternoon, playing until her hands were so sore they had to be taped."

Work — hard work — is the lot that God intended for all of us in this life.

It is only through unremitting effort and sacrifice that most people achieve success in this life or the next. In a particular way, one who works for the common good of all must, as a great poet said, "scorn delights, and live laborious days." Yet paradoxically enough, one who does that experiences the real joy of living.

The kingdom of heaven has suffered violence, and the violent take it by force. (Mt. 11:12)

Almighty God, grant that as Your Son gave an example of diligence in His work as the Carpenter of Nazareth, so might we follow His example in working for the common good.

There's Good in Everyone

"There is no surprise more magical than the surprise of being loved," Charles Morgan once said. "It is the finger of God on a man's shoulder."

There's a bit of nobility in the worst of human beings because all are made in God's image and that image can never be completely effaced or lost.

Even the person who has decided to have nothing whatsoever to do with God isn't frozen in that state of mind. Deep in the roots of his being — just because he is created in the Divine image — there is an ever-present tug toward his Maker.

It is the privilege of Christians to help him become aware of this tremendous attraction. They can honestly say to anyone with little danger of hurting their feelings, "There's a lot of good in you!" With a kind word or a friendly glance they can do much to inspire confidence. They never write anybody off!

No matter how desperate the case, no matter how ignoble the character, theirs is the unshakable conviction that there is always hope!

By this all men will know that you are My disciples, if you have love for one another. (Jn. 13:35)

O Lord, help us to see Your image in each human being and to love him or her because they were made by You and for You.

A Significant Distinction

Arnold Lunn once wrote that there are two kinds of democracy, making a distinction that gives us much food for reflection.

There is, as he put it, the democracy of the saint, which is based on compassion and humility and says, "You're as good as I am."

Opposed to that is the democracy of the sinner, which is based on envy and has as its slogan: "I'm as good as you are."

The words of these two mottoes are similar, but what a difference there is in the meaning. If we believe in an abstract principle like democracy, we can best show what we believe by our actions. A person who does nothing is likely to believe in nothing; a person with an important idea will be inspired by that idea.

Our democracy wasn't built by the lazy or the indifferent.

My soul takes pleasure in three things, and they are beautiful in the sight of the Lord and of men: agreement between brothers, friendship between neighbors, and a wife and husband who live in harmony. (Sir. 25:1)

Help me, Lord, never to fall prey to the easy way of indifference; but grant that I may ever choose the harder way of continual effort for good.

Everybody Counts

William L. Stidger, in the magazine "Your Life," told a story about the conductor Walter Damrosch. Once he stopped his orchestra when everything was apparently going along smoothly, and asked: "Where is the seventh flute? Where is the seventh flute?"

As Stidger pointed out, the conductor didn't ask for the first flute, or the second — but the seventh. Even the seventh flute had an important place in creating the harmony the leader desired.

"We may feel inferior, untalented, not even beautiful, and some of us uneducated," Stidger commented, "but each of us has a part to play and should play it well."

He told how he used to watch the man who plays the triangle in a large orchestra. Often the player would sit through the entire number, eagerly waiting. Then, toward the close, he would, with perfect timing, deftly touch the instrument and produce just the right note.

In other words, there is no really unimportant job. We should do well whatever it is our part to do.

We, though many, are one body in Christ, and individually members one of another. (Rom. 12:5)

Lord, may we always be aware that the part we play in life, however small, is important.

Collect for What?

A rare collection of bronzes was auctioned off some years ago in New York. The collection was one of the best in the world. The owner had spent 25 years of care and more than $1 million in gathering it.

The one and only heir, his wife, was bequeathed thousands of bronzes which meant nothing to her; she much preferred a modest collection of greenbacks.

With well trained indifference the auctioneer sold the 200 lots, scattering the work of a lifetime in a few hours and for a fraction of their worth.

So many of the things on which we lavish our energy, laudable as they may be in themselves, are often scattered at our death as easily as a child's wooden blocks. It seems good sense then, instead of playing with the wooden blocks of this life, to lay up indestructible treasures in the next.

Lay up for yourselves treasures in heaven, where neither moth nor rust consumes and where thieves do not break in and steal. (Mt. 6:20)

May we always remember where our true treasure lies — in and with You, Christ, for all eternity.

Let Your Love Be Known

I met a woman a while ago who had only one complaint against her husband. Seen in the perspective of a lifetime, perhaps it isn't an important one, but small things sometimes loom large in their everyday context.

"My husband always praises me to other people," she said. "Constantly I hear from friends the wonderful things he has said about me.

"But I miss something, because he never gets around to saying these things to me, to my face."

This complaint shows something about daily life. We all tend to let those we love take our love for granted. We forget that everyone has a need to be assured that they are loved.

> **A good wife . . . is far more precious than jewels. (Prov. 31:10)**

> *Lord, help husbands to praise their wives sincerely and without flattery.*

No Time to Lose

The ship's chief engineer, coming down the companion-way into the engine room, shouted: "How long have you been working in this compartment?"

The fireman, recently assigned to the crew, answered honestly: "Ever since I saw you coming down the ladder."

There is a constant temptation for all of us to "take it easy" until an emergency arises.

Often we tend to excuse our own spiritual idleness, putting off action to some future time which we imagine will be more opportune.

We are naturally inclined to believe that a kind of routine goodness is enough, and we postpone any really energetic spiritual activity. In actuality every day is the right day for spiritual labor. Every day is the proper time for directing our moral energies toward our eternal goal. Indeed, there is no time to lose!

Now is the acceptable time; behold now is the day of salvation. (2 Cor. 6:2)

May we ever be alert to serving You and the common good, O Christ.

Adversity Doesn't Kill

Three hundred years ago a prisoner condemned to the Tower of London carved on the wall of his cell this sentiment to keep up his spirits during his long imprisonment:

"It is not adversity that kills, but the impatience with which we bear adversity."

Rebelling against difficulties or obstacles that cannot legitimately be avoided only makes a bad situation worse.

Ordinary common sense recommends that we ride the storm, not buck it. But going one step further — going from the natural to the supernatural — makes it easier still to bear adversity patiently.

Once you recognize that your suffering can actually bear fruit if you try to have the same purpose as Christ, there will be joy.

Accept whatever is brought upon you, and in changes that humble you be patient. (Sir. 2:4)

Lord, give me Your grace that I may bear patiently what must be accepted for Your sake.

Clothesline Saves Baby

A clothesline saved the life of 18-month-old Judith Dehan of Chicago.

The infant unwittingly performed an acrobatic stunt that probably neither she nor circus experts could duplicate.

Tumbling from the second floor of her home, Judith fell directly onto a clothesline, strung six feet above the ground. After taking a big bounce on it, she landed unhurt in her own baby carriage. When her mother reached her she was not even crying.

The Lord protects children against all sorts of physical and spiritual harm.

But He does delegate part of this divine responsibility to parents and teachers. Do what you can to cooperate with the Creator in providing in all ways for children.

Are not two sparrows sold for a penny? Yet not one of them will fall to the ground without Your Father's will . . . Fear not, therefore; you are of more value than many sparrows. (Mt. 10:29,31)

Grant, O Lord, that we may be privileged to serve the best interests of youth.

You Can't Win

An English comedian once wrote in the London Daily Sketch the following analysis of the money problem:

"If a man runs after money, he's money mad;

"If he keeps it, he's a capitalist;

"If he spends it, he's a playboy;

"If he doesn't get it, he lacks ambition.

"If he gets it without working for it, he's a parasite;

"And if he accumulates it after a lifetime of hard work, people call him a fool who never got anything out of life."

It is true that people say all these things. In fact, when you think about it, you'll find that almost anybody can be criticized for anything.

The cure? Make sure which is the right course, then follow it, without bothering about what others may say. If you are in the right, their criticism should only be a further incentive.

What your eyes have seen do not hastily bring into court; for what will you do . . . when your neighbor puts you to shame? . . . Do not disclose another's secret; lest he who hears you bring shame upon you, and your ill repute have no end. (Prov. 25:8)

Lord, let me be merciful in my judgment of myself and others lest I be harshly judged.

Lincoln's Words Still Inspire

The writings of Abraham Lincoln are a rich mine of inspiration. Nearly every speech he made contains evidence of his deep sense of responsibility to God. And it is not hard to see why, since Lincoln himself was constantly seeking higher guidance for his thoughts and actions.

In his famous speech at Baltimore on April 18, 1864, he gave an example of this feeling of dedication when he said: "I am responsible . . . to the American people, to the Christian world, to history, and on my final account to God."

An even more famous reference to the Deity occurs in the last sentence of his immortal Gettysburg Address. The initial draft of this speech, however, did not include the words "under God." It was only as he was actually delivering his address that he spontaneously put them in. It was as if he suddenly sensed the incompleteness of his remarks and, with that last and most meaningful addition, gave his speech — and our country — its proper direction.

". . . and that this nation, under God, shall have a new birth of freedom — and that government of the people, by the people, for the people, shall not perish from the earth."

The Lord Himself created wisdom; He saw her and apportioned her . . . upon all His works. (Sir. 1:9)

God, help us to recognize that ultimately we are responsible to you.

What Time Can Not Destroy

When Daniel Webster, the great statesman and orator, spoke at Faneuil Hall, Boston, in 1852, he underlined the great service teachers render to the human community:

"If we work upon marble, it will perish.

"If we work upon brass, time will efface it.

"If we rear temples, they will crumble to dust.

"But if we work upon men's immortal minds,

"If we imbue them with high principles,

"With the just fear of God and love of their fellow man,

"We engrave on those tablets something which no time can efface,

"And which will brighten and brighten to all eternity."

Those who take up a career in teaching with a sense of devotion and dedication that makes their seemingly difficult task manageable clearly recognize that purpose makes the difference.

> **(God's) gifts were that some should be . . . teachers, to equip the saints for the work of ministry, for building up the body of Christ. (Eph. 4:11-12)**

> *Divine Teacher, send devoted and dedicated teachers into today's classrooms.*

In Marriage, There's Give and Take

St. Valentine's Day is a good day to reflect on the sacredness of the marriage bond. A portion from the lesson preceding the wedding ceremony, for instance, is worth a bit of prayerful contemplation because in it is a reminder that there is a "give" as well as "take" in every happy marriage.

"And so you begin your married life by the voluntary and complete surrender of your individual lives in the interest of that deeper and wider life which you are to have in common. Henceforth you will belong entirely to each other; you will be one in mind, one in heart, and one in affections. And whatever sacrifices you may hereafter be required to make to preserve this mutual life, always make them generously.

"Sacrifice is usually difficult and irksome. Only love can make it easy; and perfect love can make it a joy. We are willing to give in proportion as we love. And when love is perfect, the sacrifice is complete.

"God so loved the world that He gave His only begotten Son; and the Son so loved us that He gave Himself for our salvation."

A man shall leave his father and mother and be joined to his wife, and the two shall become one flesh . . . (Mk. 10:7)

Creator, endow couples with that sacrificial love which will enable them to cooperate with You in ensuring the stability of their union.

Ideals for Young People

The oath taken by the young men of Athens more than 20 centuries ago could well be followed by today's young men and women. It reads as follows:

"We will never bring disgrace to this our city by any act of dishonesty or cowardice;

"We will fight for our ideals and the sacred things of the city both alone and with many;

"We will revere and obey the city's laws and do our best to incite a like respect and reverence in those about us;

"We will strive unceasingly to quicken the public's sense of civic duty;

"In all these ways we will strive to transmit this city to others not less but greater, better and more beautiful than it was transmitted to us."

The high standards set by the young people of ancient Athens should be even bettered by the young of modern times who are blessed by God with advantages of divine revelation and freedom that few in the historic past ever enjoyed.

You are the salt of the earth; but if salt has lost its taste, how shall its saltness be restored? It is no longer good for anything except to be thrown out and trodden under foot. (Mt. 5:13)

Let us show by our actions, O divine Savior, that we appreciate the blessings of liberty.

The Power of the Pen

"I think we'll have a good potato crop this year," a newspaper editor said one morning.

"No such thing," a woman asserted. "I think the crop will be poor."

Ignoring her remark, the editor proceeded to have his estimate of the crop situation inserted on the commodities page of the evening edition of his paper.

The next day he met the same woman. She had a sheepish grin on her face and a copy of the previous day's paper in her hand. "I was wrong," she said apologetically. "It says right here in the paper that the crop will be excellent this fall."

It's human nature to believe more readily what you see in print than what you learn by word of mouth. But it's also human nature to read uncritically.

It is possible to learn to be a critical reader, to form your own opinions about topics. And the first step is to read about the same topic in newspapers and/or magazines with very different points of view.

Give Your servant therefore an understanding mind . . . that I may discern between good and evil. (1 Kgs. 3:9)

Spirit of God, give me the knowledge and wisdom to make intelligent judgments.

God's Loving Care

During a heavy storm at sea a nervous passenger on a large ship went to the captain, seeking reassurance. "Captain," he asked tremulously, "are we in great danger?"

"Don't worry . . . we are in the hands of God."

"Oh," he gasped, terror written on his face, "is it as bad as that?"

We are always in the hands of God, whether or not the weather is stormy. It is as good as that! Sometimes we forget God's presence until the last moment, until we feel the storm around us. We should be aware, even during the calm, of the bouying support of Christ.

A great storm of wind arose, and the waves beat into the boat, so that the boat was already filling. But He was in the stern, asleep . . . They woke Him . . . "Teacher, do You not care if we perish?" And He awoke and rebuked the wind, and said to the sea, "Peace! Be still!" And . . . there was a great calm. (Mk. 4:37-39)

In you, O Lord, I place all my hope and trust.

The Goodness of God

Several years ago an elderly lady made a generous gift to the poor. When asked if she could really afford it, her answer was memorable.

"I'm 74 now," she said. "My husband — God rest his soul! — died 23 years ago. He wasn't able to leave me much money, so for all this time I've earned a living by scrubbing and washing.

"But I felt I should do more than that. I wanted to help those worse off than I am. God has been good to me. I have my health, a roof over my head, enough to eat. So many people don't have these blessings.

"And then I thought it would be better to work a little bit harder in this life and take my rest in the life to come."

It's interesting to note that those who take things "a little bit harder in this life" often seem to have a foretaste of heaven here below.

Each day there are ways to be generous to others in gratitude for what you have — and it need not always involve money. Time can be more costly and therefore more clearly express your gratitude.

> **O give thanks to the Lord, for He is good; for His steadfast love endures for ever! (Ps. 107:1)**

> *Lord, help me to choose the harder path that leads to You.*

Willing to Help

In the Revolutionary War, during preparations for a battle, a man in civilian clothes passed a corporal who was arrogantly ordering his men to lift a heavy beam.

The man stopped and asked the corporal, "Why don't you help them?"

"Sir," the answer came back indignantly, "I am a corporal!"

With a muttered apology, the stranger stripped off his coat and pitched in to help the soldiers. "Mr. Corporal," he said when the task was done, "whenever you haven't enough men to do a job, call on your commander in chief. I'll be glad to help." With that, George Washington put on his coat and left.

To help others we must often humble ourselves; but, paradoxically enough, we always win by doing so. The best proof of this is Christ Himself. He became the friend and servant of the lowest among men, lepers and beggars and thieves. And for this all mankind reveres Him.

He who is greatest among you shall be your servant. (Mt. 23:11)

Lord, help me to remember that in the measure I humble myself, in Your Name, for others, You will exalt me in Your presence.

Beauty We Do Not See

Two blind beggars on a busy midwestern street were soliciting alms from the hurrying passers-by.

Both were pitiful figures, yet one of them, strangely enough, seemed to be having much more success than the other. The nickels and dimes poured into his cup, while people walked past the first beggar with hardly a glance.

An interested observer of the scene finally discovered the reason. Instead of the usual card reading, "I am blind," the successful mendicant's card read: "It is May and I am blind."

He attracted the attention of the passers-by with this reminder of the beauty of a spring he could not see — a beauty that perhaps he feared they were missing. Deprived of sight, he could understand how much of the world goes unseen by almost everyone.

Many of us live with a blindness that is not physical, unaware of the grandeur of the Creator's bounty in the world that lies around us.

Seeing they do not see, and hearing they do not hear, nor do they understand. (Mt. 13:13)

Creator, help us to see Your reflected beauty in the work of Your hands.

One Day at a Time

A man on a hiking trip through the Blue Ridge Mountains one time came to the top of a hill and saw, just below the crest, a small log cabin.

Its aged owner was sitting in front of the door, smoking a corncob pipe. When the traveler drew close enough he asked the old man patronizingly, "Lived here all your life?"

"Nope," the old mountaineer replied patiently, "not yet."

However long or short it may be, there is time ahead for all of us to live our days with purpose. When we lose this sense of purpose in life, we have lost an important part of life itself.

Do not be anxious about tomorrow, for tomorrow will be anxious for itself. Let the day's own troubles be sufficient for the day. (Mt. 6:34)

Lord, help me be ever aware that each day is a lifetime to be lived for Christ, with Christ and in Christ.

The Last Thread

In a New York court a desperate father whose son was being tried as a juvenile delinquent openly confessed that despite all that had been done for the boy — and he and his wife thought they had done almost everything possible — it had all been in vain.

"Your Honor," the father said finally, "we'll have to give the boy up — disown him. I don't see what else we can do."

"If you desert your son now," the judge told him, "you'll lose him forever. You'll break the last thread of hope — his faith in you. Without that faith, he'll be hopeless."

Rejection of those who offend us solves nothing. It doesn't help the offender; and it doesn't help us, either, since we invariably suffer. If Christ does not disown sinners, surely we can follow His example.

If any one has caused pain . . . you should rather turn to forgive and comfort him. (2 Cor. 2:5)

Lord, before I reject anyone as "lost" remind me that I have not done everything I could for that person.

The Secret of Success

"May I ask you the secret of success?" an ambitious young man said to a successful merchant.

"There is no easy or simple secret," the merchant answered. "You must be on the alert for little things and jump at opportunities."

"But how can I tell the opportunities when they come?"

"You can't," the merchant said tartly. "You just have to keep jumping."

Every day presents us with countless opportunities for success in this life and in eternity. More often than not we let them pass, judging them too small to be important. But no situation is unimportant or small if we see it clearly and make proper use of it.

Look to yourselves, that you may not lose what you have worked for, but may win a full reward. (2 Jn. 1:8)

May we be constantly alive to each opportunity to do Your will, God.

The Basis of Harmony

When he was conductor of the New York Philharmonic Orchestra, Artur Rodzinski said: "In our orchestra we have many nationalities, types, and temperaments. We have learned to forget individual likes, dislikes, and differences of temperament for the sake of music to which we have dedicated our lives.

"I often wonder if we could not solve the world's problems on a similar basis of harmony."

"Think what a single individual in a symphony orchestra can accomplish," the famous maestro continued, "by giving up his individual traits and ambitions in the service of music. . . .

"Suppose that in life you had the same all-embracing love for the whole of mankind and for your neighbor in particular. Only when everyone of us and every nation learns the secret of love for all mankind will the world become a great orchestra, following the beat of the Greatest Conductor of all."

Not until all look up to the "Greatest Conductor of all," giving Him their devotion and wholehearted love, will they learn the "secret of love for all mankind."

> (Since) you have put on the new nature . . . there cannot be Greek and Jew, circumcised and uncircumcised, barbarian, Scythian, slave, free man, but Christ is all, and in all. (Col. 3:10-11)

God, help me by my life to teach that there can be no family of humankind without the recognition of Your paternity.

Job Well Done Pays Dividends

A man who spent 27 years as a college professor once received an unexpected tribute.

An anonymous ex-student of his donated a scholarship in his honor. The ex-student, a housewife and mother, wrote a heartfelt explanatory letter saying that as a result of her studies under this professor ". . . my life has been enriched in many ways. Inner resources have been built up, friendships have been found, and most important of all, I have been better equipped for the job of motherhood."

After describing the teacher's fine qualities, the donor said: "It seems to me that a teacher who is able to direct the hidden springs of energy into a constructive path on the part of his students, who is able without distortion or drama to give a fuller life to people he is guiding, is indeed a great man."

We can all be stimulated by the example of this teacher, who produced such a wonderful and far-reaching effect simply by doing his job well and sincerely. That is an achievement within the reach of us all.

I can do all things in Him who strengthens me. (Phil. 4:13)

Give me the will to do what You will, Father.

A Role for Everyone

A bricklayer whose brother happened to be a gifted and famous violinist once found himself in conversation with the head of the construction company for which he worked.

"It must be fine to have such a renowned man for a brother," the executive observed. And then, anxious not to offend his worker's pride, he continued:

"Of course we must accept the fact that talent isn't evenly distributed — even in the same family."

"That's the truth," came back the reply. "Why, my brother doesn't know the first thing about bricklaying. It's a good thing he can afford to pay others to build his house for him."

It's not vanity to recognize our own place in life and our fitness for it. Instead of wasting our time envying others we should devote ourselves to the productive use of our own ability. God intends each of us for a special job.

Well done, good and faithful servant! You have been faithful over a little, I will set You over much. Enter into the joy of your master. (Mt. 25:23)

Lord, help me to appreciate the talents You have given me.

Sympathy Conquers All

In one of the battles of the Civil War when his army was suffering a severe defeat, Gen. Robert E. Lee rode over a section of the battlefield where the fighting had passed on. As he did so, a wounded Northern soldier in the spirit of defiance lifted his head and shouted: "Hurrah for the Union."

The soldier then expected to be shot, but instead Lee dismounted and said simply, "I'm sorry that you are so gravely wounded. I hope you may soon be well."

Afterward the soldier said: "That spirit broke my heart, and I cried myself to sleep."

Often others are hateful to us only because they expect unkindness and are anticipating it. When they receive instead a word or a gesture of friendship, they are defenseless and quickly ready to return the kindness they are given.

Just as hatred breeds hatred, so love creates love.

Love your enemies, do good to them that hate you. (Lk. 6:27)

Give me, Lord, an understanding sympathy even for those who mistakenly hate me.

Returning to Our Origin

At the beginning of the lenten season it is appropriate to consider our origin. We indeed had a humble beginning for, as the writer of the book of Genesis says, "the Lord God formed man of dust from the ground . . ." (Gen. 2:7) That is why on Ash Wednesday our foreheads are smudged with ashes for we "are dust, and to dust (we) shall return." (Gen. 3:19)

But more important is the rest of the creation narrative: ". . . and breathed into his nostrils the breath of life; and man became a living being." (Gen. 2:7)

Lent is the time to return to Him in whose image we are made. We do this by putting God first in our lives, by living out the lifestyle His Son, Jesus, gave us.

It is a joyous thing to realize that we are created by God in His image and filled with His Spirit. That we are "living beings" — beings with souls — makes it possible for us to cooperate with God in the development of His life within us.

Return to the Lord, your God, for He is gracious and merciful. (Joel 2:13)

Merciful Lord, help me to change my lifestyle in at least one area this Lent.

Inner Conflicts Affect Your Teeth

Do you gnash your teeth? If you do, it may be a sign that you are under too much stress or are emotionally upset.

This conclusion was reached by one dentist after considerable research on the subject.

The doctor also pointed out that clenching and grinding your teeth leads to many troubles. The habit causes teeth to rock in their sockets. This in turn leads to gum inflammation, gum disease and eventual damage to underlying bones.

Inner conflicts are the root cause of much more harm than the grinding of teeth. When a person's spiritual life is out of kilter, it invariably affects his whole make-up of body and soul.

Keep your mind, heart and spirit in the serene, well-balanced condition that God wishes for each of us and you will radiate your inner joy into the lives of countless others. There will be little danger of being tortured by your own pent-up tensions.

If you had walked in the way of God, you would be dwelling in peace for ever. (Bar. 3:13)

Grant, O Father, that I may be Your instrument in helping those weighed down by sadness.

Not Licked Yet

A man walking along the street passed a vacant lot where some boys were playing baseball. He asked one of the youngsters what the score was.

"We're behind, 18 to 0," was the answer.

"Well," said the man, "I must say you don't look very discouraged."

"Discouraged?" the boy said, puzzled. "We're not discouraged. We haven't come to bat yet!"

There is a thought in this anecdote that could cheer us all: on those days when life seems to be defeating us, when small trials come in a series, we can think of life as a kind of baseball game, and patiently wait our turn at bat. Moreover, we can have the confidence of a winning team, since we have a Captain incapable of failure.

In all these things we are more than conquerors through Him who loved us. (Rom. 8:37)

God, give me the confidence which comes from implicit trust in You.

The Disease of Avarice

"Avarice and luxury have been the ruin of every great state" warned Livy, one of Rome's greatest historians.

The downfall of any nation, even the most powerful, really begins where person after person falls victim to greed and miserliness — the deadly symptoms of avarice.

The corrosive effects of this inordinate lust for material things reach into every aspect of life, and once entrenched, are almost impossible to extricate.

As an old French proverb runs: "Long after other sins are old, avarice remains young."

There is little danger that avarice will ever get a grip on you if you strive to be the opposite of greedy and miserly.

To help you, God has given you an inborn sense of divine balance. He expects you to work constantly to help others less fortunate to acquire the basic necessities and comforts of life that you would seek if you were in their circumstances.

For the love of money is the root of all evils; it is through this craving that some have wandered away from the faith and pierced their hearts with many pangs. (1 Tim. 6:10)

Keep me, O Jesus, from avarice by being alert to the needs of others.

Get Off the Shelf

A little cake of yeast on the kitchen shelf can teach a big lesson. Its power to turn inert dough into wholesome, palatable bread is a graphic reminder of the dynamic potential within you.

For centuries yeast had been a source of wonder and speculation. But it was not until 1857 that Louis Pasteur painstakingly proved that its transforming powers stem from the fact that it is a living organism.

He conclusively demonstrated that a living thing must always be the starting point for the production of more living matter.

As the "live" cake of yeast must be in the midst of inert dough to do its energizing work, you too must get off the shelf and into the midst of things to be effective.

Think of yourself as a bit of divine yeast with God-given power to leaven the modern world with divine love, truth and justice.

Lift up your eyes, and see how the fields are already white for harvest. (Jn. 4:35)

Permit me, O Savior, to play a role, however insignificant, in transforming the world.

Murder in the Library

When the librarian saw a youngster who was scarcely tall enough to look over her desk, she leaned over and asked: "What can I do for you?"

The boy moved up a little closer and replied in a loud whisper: "Got any murders?"

Children are naturally attracted to reading and recreation that is exciting. But care should be taken to see that they don't get an overdose of it. A lack of such balance hinders many a youngster from achieving a well-rounded development.

It is not easy to foster in children habits that contribute to their intellectual, spiritual and emotional fulfillment.

But parents, teachers, librarians and all others entrusted by God with molding youthful hearts, minds and souls should count it a challenging privilege to play any part in bringing out the great potential hidden in every child.

Hear . . . instruction, and be attentive, that you may gain insight. (Prov. 4:1)

Bless all those who strive to bring out the best in children, O Lord.

You Get as You Give

High up in the Rockies there lived a small boy and his mother. One day, after he had been punished severely, the lad ran to the edge of a precipice and shouted back at his mother, "I hate you! I hate you!"

Across the ravine came the echo: "I hate you! I hate you!"

Thoroughly frightened, the boy ran back to his mother, and sobbed: "Who is that bad man over there who shouted, 'I hate you'?"

Taking the boy's hand, the mother led him back to the edge of the precipice. "Now, sonny," she said, "call out, 'I love you! I love you!'"

The little boy did as he was told. Clearly and sweetly the echo came, repeating his words.

"My child," said the mother, taking the child into her arms, "that is the law of life — what you give, you get."

Cast your bread upon the waters for you will find it after many days. (Prov. 11:1)

O Lord, teach me to be as interested in giving as I am in getting.

Unjust Landlord Jailed

For the 83rd time, a landlord was found guilty of depriving his tenants of their rights.

For the last two offenses of failing to provide sufficient heat in two of his 25 tenements, he was given 30 days in jail and fined $400.

The magistrate denounced the defendant as "irresponsible" and "unscrupulous" and "a cruel man causing anguish and grief and suffering to many families for one thing and one thing only — money."

The judge then added: "There is something radically wrong with the system when an owner of 15 buildings is convicted for making life miserable and difficult for hundreds of rent-paying men and women, and particularly little children, and nothing is done to him other than the payment of fines, which no doubt he considers ordinary business expenses like paying the salary of a janitor."

Protecting innocent victims against the few who might defraud them is a holy work. In God's divine plan there can be no peace without justice.

The memory of the righteous is a blessing, but the name of the wicked will rot. (Prov. 10:7)

Help me, O Holy Spirit, to champion the God-given rights of the poor and afflicted.

A Second Chance

In the Academy at Florence one of the great Italian masterpieces displayed is Michelangelo's statue "David." Yearly thousands of people admire this early example of the great master's work, unaware that the huge block of stone from which the figure was hewn has a curious history.

At first an inferior artist began to work on it, but through lack of skill, he succeeded only in hacking and marring the marble. Then the rulers of Florence called on the young Michelangelo, who created a lasting work of art.

There is no one so ruined that he is undeserving of a second chance. As the true artist saw in the shapeless mass of stone the outline of his masterpiece, so God sees in the lowest of the low that unextinguished spark of goodness and humanity which can be his salvation.

All of us can do the same, looking at everyone in a creative, not destructive, spirit. God will guide us in the good work of restoring what was lost, of giving life to what was spiritually dead.

It is not the will of My Father who is in heaven that one of these little ones should perish. (Mt. 18:14)

O Lord, as you have so often given me a second chance grant that I may always help others to have their second chance.

'Fantastic' Burglary Nets $50,000

Safe-crackers showed a determination and thoroughness worthy of a far better cause when they stole $50,000 in Miami.

The police had only one word for the burglary — "fantastic." The thieves smashed two large safes to get at the money, knocking down a warehouse wall in the process.

They rolled two other safes out on dollies and packed them into a truck. Apparently they came equipped with an electric drill. The whole job was estimated by police to have taken a good five hours.

All this time the night watchman was asleep in the room above. It was his first evening on the job.

"I didn't hear a thing," he told authorities.

The forces of evil don't stand a chance when good people are wide awake and do what they are supposed to. Otherwise the initiative goes by default to the unscrupulous.

Those who love God and their fellow men should use as much ingenuity to save the world as others do to wreck it.

The sons of this world are more shrewd in dealing with their own generation than the sons of light. (Lk. 16:8)

Alert me, O Lord, to the harsh realities of life, so that I may turn them into opportunities.

The Greater Fool

An English nobleman gave a jester a wand, saying: "Keep this until you find a greater fool than yourself." The jester laughingly accepted the wand and flourished it on festive occasions.

One day the nobleman lay dying. Calling the jester to his bedside, he said: "I am going on a long journey." "Where to?" asked the jester. "I don't know," came the reply.

"How long will you be gone?" asked the jester. "I shall be gone forever," came the reply. "What provisions have you made for the trip?" the jester asked. The nobleman shrugged his shoulders. "None at all."

"Then," said the jester, "take this." And placing the wand in the nobleman's hands, he added: "It belongs to you."

Those who fail to realize the purpose of life — where they came from and where they are going — are running a foolish risk. You can help them out of their predicament by praying for them and by "going" to them with the love that Christ has given to you.

The fool says in his heart, "There is no God." They are corrupt, they do abominable deeds, there is none that does good. (Ps. 14:1)

Lord, let me not fail to make provision for the long journey.

Face the Facts

Some time ago a Minneapolis woman gave her life's savings to a persuasive crook when she was assured the money would be profitably invested in a legitimate business concern.

Naturally, the swindler skipped town and left no trace of his whereabouts. When the woman reported the case to the city's Better Business Bureau, one of the bureau officials interrupted her tale of woe with this question: "Why didn't you come to us first? Obviously you knew about our service."

"Yes, I knew all right," was the astonishing answer, "but I was afraid if I told you what I intended to do, you'd tell me not to do it!"

Everywhere it's the same old story. People refuse to face facts because they are afraid that knowledge of the truth will make demands upon them. Yet a moment of serious reflection should convince them that it is the truth which protects them and saves them from the misery of disillusionment.

Know the truth, and the truth will make you free. (Jn. 8:32)

Lord, give us a courageous love of truth.

Danger of Compromising

A cartoon in a national humor magazine amused me very much. The drawing showed a self-satisfied-looking man and his wife leaving church on a bright Sunday morning.

"Everything considered," the man was declaring, "he preaches remarkably good sermons. It's so hard to avoid offending people like us."

While it is true that "honey catches more flies than vinegar," we should, at all costs, avoid making compromises with what we believe to be right.

In the long run people will respect us more for dignified disagreement with them than for any kind of fawning agreement.

> **If you really fulfill the royal law, according to the scripture, "You shall love your neighbor as yourself," you do well. But if you show partiality, you commit sin. (Jas. 2:8-9)**

> *Lord, let me not be too weak to respect my own point of view or so obstinate as to belittle that of others.*

A Little Knowledge

A high school girl, seated next to a famous astronomer at a dinner party, struck up a conversation with him asking: "What do you do for a living?"

"I study astronomy," he replied.

"Really?" said the teenager, wide-eyed. "I finished astronomy last year."

Many people stop growing mentally and spiritually at an early age. Physically, they continue to develop, but otherwise they remain six-year-olds. Yet most of us — like the famous English writer and teacher who had the habit of listing his occupation always as "student" — do recognize that we have a lot to learn, especially in those things which concern us spiritually.

The words and actions of other people are one of the best sources of learning. By appreciating those around us, by realizing how much one can share with them and gain from them, we inevitably grow daily in knowledge and in love.

> **Wisdom cries aloud in the street; in the markets she raises her voice; on the top of the walls she cries out; at the entrance of the city gates she speaks. (Prov. 1:20-21)**

O Lord, help me to grow each day in knowledge and love of others.

Every Act a Prayer

As we were sitting in the office of a busy college president one day, our eye was caught by a little framed plaque with an interesting saying on it. It was almost hidden behind a row of books, so as to be invisible to the casual visitor but constantly in the view of the man behind the desk.

Here are words that this president made it a point to keep before him all through his day's work. The plaque read:

"Lord, I shall be verie busie this day. I may forget Thee, but do not Thou forget me."

These are the words of Sir Jacob Astley's memorable prayer before the battle of Newbury. This simple thought suggests an important principle: by directing our "intention" we can make our every act a prayer. Thus our daily tasks are made more meaningful and more rewarding as well.

Whatever you do, in word or deed, do everything in the name of the Lord Jesus, giving thanks to God the Father through Him. (Col. 3:17)

Lord, help me to make my every act a prayer.

Spark of Genius

A gifted artist, walking in the countryside, saw a small boy painting on a flat rock, while his sheep browsed nearby. The boy was using cheap colors and a homemade brush yet his painting showed unmistakable talent.

The artist took the boy under his wing, fostered and taught him. The spark of genius burst into a flame and the boy became one of the world's most renowned painters.

We often hear people complain, "If only I were talented!" "How I would love to play the piano!" "I wish I had his abilities!" and so on. And they waste their lives in useless wishing, envy, and self-frustration. Yet actually they may possess the talent they envy in others.

Potentiality is never known except in action. If we would only make a start, we might find we had the potentiality. And if we continue to act, often we will build up the ability we desire.

A desire fulfilled is sweet to the soul. (Prov. 13:19)

Lord, whatever I do, give me the spirit to do it well.

Sheep Wired for Sound

Farmers in Australia have a device to help them keep in close contact with their widely scattered sheep.

A tiny radio transmitter is attached to the back of the sturdiest sheep in a flock. Through it, the periodic "bleep" is relayed to the farmer on his direction-finder set.

Since sheep always follow their leader, there is little chance that many of them will go far astray without being quickly located.

Another advantage of keeping sheep "on the air" is that help can be quickly rushed to flocks in need. Up to 25 percent of the 40 million lambs born every year in Australia die within the first few months, so this should mean a great saving.

Science is benefiting both man and beast in many ways. But it is even more deeply satisfying to realize that the Good Shepherd is in constant contact with each of us in all our wandering through life, and is ever ready to help us.

I am the Good Shepherd; I know My own and My own know Me. (Jn. 10:14)

Thank you, Lord, for keeping watch over me no matter how far I may stray.

Christt Be With Me

Over 1,500 years ago St. Patrick composed this famous prayer, "The Breastplate," before beginning his missionary work among the Irish. It has stirred the hearts of millions ever since.

"Christ be with me, Christ in the front,
"Christ in the rear, Christ within me,
"Christ below me, Christ above me,
"Christ at my right hand, Christ at my left,
"Christ in the fort, Christ in the chariot seat,
"Christ at the helm,
"Christ in the heart of every man who thinks of me,
"Christ in the mouth of every man who speaks to me,
"Christ in every eye that sees me,
"I bind to myself this day
"The strong faith of the Invocation of the Trinity,
"The faith of the Trinity in Unity.
"The Creator of the Elements,
"Salvation is the Lord's,
"Salvation is from Christ,
"Thy Salvation, O Lord, be with us forever."

Do we ask God to be with us at the start of each day's work?

I love You, O Lord, my strength . . . my rock, and my fortress, and my deliverer. (Ps. 18:1)

Christ, Son of the living God, be with us!

Playing It Too Safe

A farmer was sitting on his porch, glumly staring into space, when a passer-by called to him: "How's your cotton this year?"

"Ain't got none," answered the farmer. "Afraid of boll weevils."

"What about your corn?"

"Season looked dry so I didn't plant none."

The stranger was puzzled. "What did you plant?"

"Nuthin," said the farmer. "I played it safe."

There are a lot of us who "play it safe" by doing nothing with our talents, by burying them and feeling righteous about it, while we watch others expose themselves to risk and failure.

But if we take the example of Christ and His apostles, we can see the error of false security. We can be safe only when we are acting boldly for Christ.

By this My Father is glorified, that you bear much fruit, and so prove to be My disciples. (Jn. 15:8)

Inspire me, O God, to will and to accomplish something in Your name.

All in the Point of View

An anonymous author has given expression to a valuable thought which calls for no comment from us:

"When the other fellow acts that way, he's ugly;
"When you do it, it's nerves.
"When he's set in his ways, he's obstinate;
"When you are, it's just firmness.
"When he doesn't like your friends, he's prejudiced;
"When you don't like his, you are simply showing good judgment of human nature.
"When he tries to be accommodating, he's polishing the apple;
"When you do it, you're using tact.
"When he takes time to do things, he is dead slow;
"When you take ages, you are deliberate.
"When he picks flaws, he's cranky;
"When you do, you're discriminating."

Judge not, and you will not be judged; condemn not, and you will not be condemned; forgive, and you will be forgiven; give and it will be given to you; . . . For the measure you give will be the measure you get back. (Lk. 7:37-38)

Jesus, give me the grace to see my own faults before I look for faults in others.

Heroism on an Elevator

Two workmen were trapped on the cab of a runaway elevator as it suddenly shot upward toward the low-hanging girders at the head of the shaft.

One of the two, a young mechanic from Brooklyn, reached over and pushed the other man flat on top of the zooming car for fear the girders would crush him. In doing so, he caught his own arm between the elevator and the shaft and was crushed to death.

The vehicle stopped its climb just one floor below the roof of the 18-story building.

Human beings achieve their greatest dignity when they forget themselves in a heroic act of love for God and their fellow human beings.

Natural and man-made disasters often provide the setting for magnificent deeds of service to humanity that surprise even those who perform them.

Don't wait for an emergency, though, before you put the divine chivalry within you to work in some practical way.

Greater love has no man than this, that a man lay down his life for his friends. (Jn. 15:13)

Let me show in thought, word and deed, O Lord, that I am willing to endure loss for the good of others.

At the Cost of Others

An ancient anecdote about Mohammed illustrates an important rule of conduct: that we should not try to advance ourselves by deprecating others. The story goes like this:

A disciple came to Mohammed one morning and said, "Master, my six brothers are all asleep and I alone have remained awake to worship Allah."

Mohammed answered him: "And you had better been asleep, if your worship of Allah consists of accusations against your brothers."

Fault-finding and magnifying the mistakes of others are poor ways of changing the world for the better. Wrongdoing, of course, has to be identified, but means to correct it should always be positive and constructive, not negative and destructive.

A Christoper — a bearer of Christ — will detest the sin but not the sinner. He will advance the cause of justice and peace and truth, yet he will not do so at the expense of the feelings of others. Always his motto will be: "Better to light one candle than to curse the darkness."

If anyone says, "I love God," and hates his brother, he is a liar; for he who does not love his brother whom he has seen, cannot love God whom he has not seen. (1 Jn. 4:20)

Guide me, O Lord, that I may never strive to rise by pushing others down.

Drop Your Buckets

An ocean vessel, limping in from the sea, dropped anchor at some distance from the mouth of a river and signaled to the shore for fresh water. Back came the answer, "Drop your buckets!"

The captain became angry, thinking it hardly the time or place for a joke. Again he signaled for water, adding, "Let's be serious about this."

Again came the answer: "Drop your buckets."

For the third time the captain signaled. When he received the same answer the third time, he ordered the buckets dipped into the water. When they were pulled up, the water was found to be fresh.

We often think that the real opportunities to develop our character, to do something big, lie far off. Actually, we need only dip our bucket into the flowing river of everyday life to find ample opportunity for service to Our Lord.

At Your word I will let down the nets. (Lk. 5:5)

Lord, help me to see my opportunities for service to You in my daily round of duty.

True Treasure

A man was walking down a dark alley, thinking his own thoughts, so he didn't notice the approach of a hold-up man until he felt a gun in his back and heard a low voice whispering:

"Your money or your life."

"Take my life," the victim replied promptly, "I'm saving my money for my old age."

Some of us not only save our money for our old age, but seem to save our lives for our old age as well.

We are reluctant to give ourselves to living, to dedicate our time and our spirit to a full life of spirit, a life that concerns itself with our neighbor, whether he is next door or half a world away.

Yet the truth is that only through this whole-hearted living do we really live at all.

Where your treasure is, there will your heart be. (Mt. 6:21)

Lord, help me to "wear out" in Your service instead of "rusting out" in self-preservation.

Living and Giving

Betsy Barton, who lost the use of both legs in an automobile crash, once said:

"It is my experience that suffering and pain are, unfortunately, the great character builders — not that suffering is good in itself, but because it often helps to shift our expectation of happiness from without to a search for it from within . . .

"Mystics, to achieve spiritual understanding, cleared the way by depriving themselves of things by their own will. But we are so suffocated with things and with distractions that the real pursuit of happiness is almost impossible . . .

"Happiness is primarily an inner state, an inner achievement . . . the Kingdom of Heaven is within us."

Suffering may be the means whereby we achieve self-understanding. In the measure that we achieve self-understanding we are able to reach out with understanding to others.

Happiness is not found in the pursuit of things or in the possession of things. It comes from living and giving, from suffering and participation in the sufferings of others.

Through many tribulations, we must enter the kingdom of God. (Acts 14:22)

Suffering Savior, may I overcome suffering, not be overcome by it.

It's God's Idea

The English novelist H. G. Wells once called upon the American novelist Henry James.

In the drawing room of James' house Wells noticed a large and peculiar stuffed bird.

"My dear James," he said, astonished, "what is that?"

"That," James replied, "is a stork."

"Humph," Wells snorted. "It's not my idea of a stork."

"Apparently, however," came the answer, "it was God's idea of one."

Frequently our idea of something may not be God's idea; subconsciously, we may even feel that our idea is better. But the Creator's plan is above our logic. When we accept it, we find ourselves quickly in tune with life, more able to act constructively, to create according to the will of God, instead of blundering along in our private confusion.

The ways of the Lord are right, and the upright walk in them, but transgressors stumble in them. (Hos. 14:10)

Give us, O Father, the wisdom to see Your ways and the courage to walk therein.

Not Alone

Admiral Byrd, on one of his trips to Little America, spent months alone, apart from his party, living in a small cabin equipped with rough furnishings. He had no companion save the fierce Antarctic storms. Single-handed, he cleaned his cabin, checked his instruments, prepared his meals.

One is tempted, reading this, to think that Admiral Byrd was self-sufficient. Yet a little thought reveals how dependent he was upon others. He needed others to get him to Antarctica; to build his cabin; to keep in touch with him by radio.

When he was dangerously ill, his men brought him medical aid. He was dependent, too, upon those who financed his project, on the farmers who raised his food, on the designers and manufacturers of his scientific instruments.

One of the weaknesses of our age is that of failing to recognize not only the social nature of man but, even more, man's dependence on God. However, each of us can do his part to restore that recognition.

None of us lives to himself, and none of us dies to himself. (Rom. 14:7)

Father of the human family, send many into the market place announcing that all are Your children and brothers and sisters of each other.

Appearances Are Deceiving

A celebrated French artist who never bothered much with his appearance was out walking one morning when he heard a feminine voice behind him call: "My good man, can you carry my bundle a little way for me?"

Turning, he saw a very beautiful woman; so, instead of explaining who he was, he said, "Most willingly, madame," and took the bundle from her.

First into one shop then into another he followed her. Finally the woman came to her home and fumbled in her purse for some change. But when she offered it to him, the artist refused.

"Madame," he said, "I am not a porter, despite the ungracious compliment you paid my appearance. I am an artist, and I shall be well repaid if I can make a copy of your beautiful face and send it to the next exhibition at the Academy."

How easy it is to take external appearances as everything. And, to carry the point still further, how easy it is to forget the image of God in each of His creatures.

Do not judge by appearances, but judge with right judgment. (Jn. 7:24)

Lord, teach me always to find Your image in others.

Double-Dealing

A small item in the New York Times told a disturbing story. "Publicity Concern Plays Both Sides in Labor Rows" was the headline; then the story went on to explain how a public relations organization in recent strikes had been engaged by opposing sides and had, on different days, given out publicity releases, some of which took violent issue with management, others which were equally violent against the unions.

Surely we all know people of whom this reminds us: those whose convictions change from one day to the next, yet they are always argumentative no matter what side they currently happen to be defending.

Being changeable is not necessarily the sign of an "open mind"; those whose convictions continually vary are likely not to have any convictions at all.

People whose lives have a basis of divine truth and belief may change their minds about the lesser things, but they remain firm at heart and quietly command the respect of others of weaker principles.

God's firm foundation stands, bearing this seal: "The Lord knows those who are His." (2 Tim. 2:19)

Author of my faith, make my faith steadfast.

Up the Steep Slopes

Someone once asked Mallory, the famous climber who lost his life on Mount Everest, why he wanted to attempt to scale that mountain. Mallory answered simply: "Because it is there."

The daring climber saw a challenge in the very existence of the uncharted peak, and something would not let him rest until he had attempted it.

Many of us would like to drift through life, taking it as it comes, following the easy path.

But for others a challenge exists — the challenge to live creatively, to mold life into something worthwhile. Like the climber, they see the difficulty and the hardship, but they see also the reward: a deep sense of accomplishment — the sense Christians have when they carry Christ up the steep slopes and keep in sight the end of the climb — the peak of eternity.

I am sure that neither death, nor life, nor angels, nor principalities, nor things present, nor things to come, nor powers, nor height, nor depth, nor anything else . . . will be able to separate us from the love of God in Christ Jesus. (Rom. 8:38-39)

Lord, teach me never to turn away from the challenge life offers to win others for You.

Do More Than Talk

The leader of a discussion group made this sweeping statement near the end of the program: "Now that we've taken care of the Far East, let's take up the Near East!"

It is a common failing to think that the complex crises of modern life can be solved merely by talking about them. If such problems could be solved by words alone, we would have had global peace long ago.

To avoid the danger of being long on words and short on "doing," encourage the members of any organizations to which you belong to spend 30 minutes of performance for every five minutes of talk.

See that your meetings get beyond the talking stage. Help to put into application the principles for which the organization stands.

God will bless you if you put your ideals to work in a specific way instead of sitting on the sidelines indulging in wishful thinking or repeating high-sounding principles.

Little children, let us not love in word or speech but in deed and in truth. (1 Jn. 3:18)

Let me be a doer of Your Word, O Lord.

Generosity Always Wins

When the car in which two teenagers were riding stalled in a busy downtown street in Madison, Wis., a sympathetic spectator offered a helping hand.

But just as the automobile began to roll, the man suddenly noticed that it was his own car that he was generously helping to push.

The young men lost no time in waking up to the same fact and rapidly took to their heels, scurrying into a nearby alley.

Never underestimate the surprising effects that come from being generous with God or man.

You always help yourself in one way or another when you strive to help others. This generous man might never have recovered his own stolen automobile so quickly if he had ignored his impulse to lend a helping hand to those who seemed to be in distress.

Give, and it will be given to you. (Lk. 6:38)

Deepen in me, Savior, a sincere desire to be as generous to others as You are with me.

Watch the Notices

A man in one of our large cities received from the Bureau of Internal Revenue a "Second Notice" that his tax payment was overdue. The notice carried with it dire threats as to what would be done if the payment was not forthcoming immediately.

Hurrying to the collector's office, the man paid up and said: "I'd have paid this before but I didn't get your first notice."

"Oh," replied the clerk, "we've run out of first notices, and besides, we find the second notices are a lot more effective."

When we think back, we can recall many "first notices" that God has given us which we have ignored; perhaps an opportunity missed or a warning not heeded brought trouble because we were just too complacent or selfish.

It's human nature to wait until the lightning has hit the roof before we take out insurance. If we're lucky enough to have a third warning, the premium has gone up so far the price that must be paid means compromise and sacrifice. The accounting will be all the more difficult when we are called.

O that today you would hearken to His voice! (Ps. 95:7)

Lord, make me alert to Your inspirations.

Think Before You Speak

A young man lying on a hospital stretcher just before his operation turned to a sympathetic woman who stood nearby and said: "I'm so nervous. This is my first operation."

"So am I," said the woman, "my husband is the doctor and it is his first operation too."

One important expression of true love for others, which this doctor's wife seems to have forgotten, is tactfulness: saying or doing what is encouraging, not discouraging; being honest without being brutal; showing a Christ-like consideration for the feelings of others (no matter how mistaken they may be); and avoiding abruptness and sarcasm.

Tactfulness is a habit which can be developed anywhere — in the home, the factory, the office, the school.

The tongue is a little member and boasts of great things. How great a forest is set ablaze by a small fire! (Jas. 3:5)

Lord, help me always to have concern for the feelings of others.

A Rich Cargo

On the docks of Gloucester, Mass., a man from the city and a grizzled fisherman were watching two vessels come home through the fog.

The first ship was high and graceful, moving easily through the sea. The second, heavy-laden and listing, groaned through the mist.

To the stranger the first ship seemed the more impressive, but to the practiced eye of the fisherman, the slow, heavy movement of the second ship meant that she contained a rich cargo, that she had dared the deep waters where the quantities of fish wait for the enterprising crew.

To many of us the shallow water may seem more attractive, the easier job more alluring, but when we "launch out into the deep" we discover that the real reward is there, in the fuller labor of spreading Christ's truth and love.

Put out into the deep and let down your nets for a catch. (Lk. 5:4)

O God, teach me to be a fisher of women and men.

Self-Reliant

The town of Teaneck, N.J., in a drive for cancer research, was astonished to learn that the most indefatigable worker was a widow who had been blind for 13 years.

This woman, however, saw nothing unusual in what she had done. "After all," she told a reporter who came to interview her, "I was taught to be self-reliant and I can distinguish between light and shadow, so I am not altogether helpless . . .

"There is much that I can do . . . and thank God I never was one to be sad. My blindness came over me gradually and I consider myself lucky to have had so many years of sight."

By praying for God's guidance, we can learn, as this remarkable woman did, to "count our blessings" and to see the good side of our situation in life, whatever it may be.

Let the peace of Christ rule in your hearts . . . And be thankful. (Col. 3:15)

Jesus, may we learn to "count our blessings."

Ready for the Worst

A doctor tells this story of an eight-year-old boy whose sister was dying of a disease from which the boy himself had recovered some time before. Realizing that only a transfusion of her brother's blood would save the little girl, the doctor asked the boy: "Would you like to give your blood for your sister?"

The child hesitated for a moment, his eyes wide with fear. Then, finally, he said: "Sure, doctor, I'll do it."

Only later, after the transfusion was completed, did the boy ask hesitantly, "Say, doctor, when do I die?" Then the doctor understood the momentary hesitation and fear. It had taken the boy that long to decide to sacrifice his life for his sister.

Heroic bravery isn't limited only to grownups or to soldiers or firemen. It takes real courage to face sacrifice, to be willing to give ourselves up for others.

The gate is narrow and the way is hard, that leads to life, and those who find it are few. (Mt. 7:14)

Jesus, give me daily the strength of soul to meet the opportunities for sacrifice in my life.

Following Their Path

Some years ago a group of five boys in Rome were exploring the ancient catacombs beneath the city. Their lantern burned up all its fuel, and for two days and two nights the boys tried in vain to find a way out.

On the third day, tired, hungry, and frightened, they began groping on their hands and knees. Suddenly they discovered smooth places worn in the rock floor of the ancient passage. It was the path followed by the early Christians, who had come there for their devotions centuries before. Feeling out this path, the boys crawled to safety and the light of day.

When we feel lost and afraid sometimes, and the darkness of daily life seems to be closing around us, we might think of those early Christians: their sacrifices, trials, and martyrdoms.

That should bring light into our darkness and give us the inspiration to set newly ablaze our own faith.

Did we not act in the same spirit? Did we not take the same steps? (2 Cor. 12:18)

Lord, give us the strength to walk the path of martyrdom in the faithful performance of our duties.

Dividing and Subdividing

The lovely flowering shrub, the fuchsia, was introduced into England by an old nurseryman who heard from a friend one day that an extraordinary flower of rich crimson and deep purple had been brought from the West Indies to a lady he knew.

This so aroused the nurseryman's curiosity that he went to the owner of the plant and, after much persuasion, bought it from her. Immediately he stripped it of flowers and buds, divided it into cuttings which he forced in hotbeds, redivided, subdivided, and cultivated with care, skill, and perseverance.

At the next flowering season his labors were well rewarded by the genuine pleasure shown by visitors to his exhibition of 300 healthy plants, which were proudly displayed in his show window.

When we have something we value, especially the blessing of faith, we may overlook what joy it would give others to possess it. Yet we should try to cultivate and develop it and strive to see that this joy may be shared by many.

Those that were sown upon the good soil are the ones who hear the word and accept it and bear fruit, thirtyfold and sixtyfold and a hundredfold. (Mk. 4:20)

May we know the joy that comes from sharing with others, Lord.

Real Courtesy

A sauntering rookie soldier from Alabama encountered a brisk second lieutenant. "Mawnin'," drawled the rookie pleasantly.

The outraged officer launched a stinging lecture on military courtesy, with emphasis on saluting.

"Shucks," said the rookie, "if I had known you were gonna carry on like that, I wouldn't of spoke to you a-tall."

The reaction of the rookie was natural enough. Most of us probably show routine courtesy to those we meet. But it is much more difficult to go out of one's way and be kind to those who are gruff in return.

Yet that should be the spirit of a Christopher — to make a special effort to be kind to those who least deserve it. More often than not, warmth and kindness, if pursued perseveringly, thaw out the frostiest of persons. In true charity, they supply what may be lacking in others.

Let brotherly love continue. (Heb. 13:1)

May we always be kind to those who fail in kindness to us, Spirit of Wisdom.

Get at the Roots

Just as he had sunk into mire up to his chin in a collapsed cesspool, a 42-year-old laborer was rescued by fellow workers on Long Island.

During a construction job, the earth had suddenly given way under him and he plunged 15 feet into the cesspool.

Slowly but surely he was being dragged down into the mire-like quicksand. It took two hours of frantic digging and pulling before the helpless man was rescued.

Few people actually fall into a cesspool. But many, especially youngsters, are being smothered and debased by the filth and slime that disfigure modern life.

Rather than bemoan the plight of those caught in the frightening trend toward brutality, indecency, and lawlessness, help to change the trend. Get at the roots.

Do something positive and constructive to provide the good home training, sound spiritual values, and the wholesome literature and entertainment that God meant all of us to enjoy.

Woe to him by whom (temptations) come! It were better for him if a millstone were hung round his neck and he were cast into the sea, than that he should cause one of these little ones to sin. (Lk. 17:1-2)

Have mercy, O Lord, on those who are the victims of moral decay.

A Story of Two Houses

A father and his five-year-old son were walking along a street in Jamaica, Long Island. Suddenly the little boy said, "Look, daddy, what an old ramshackle house!"

The father seized the opportunity to teach his son a lesson in personal responsibility. "Yes, it certainly is, son. See how dirty it is, how the shutters look as though they're about to fall off, how the floor boards on the porch are all rotted.

"Now, do you remember the lovely Rufus King house I showed you the other day? That house was built long before this — way back before Washington was our first president, in fact. Yet the Rufus King house is in very good condition . . . and do you know why?

"Because people have taken care of it these past 200 years, while the people who lived in this house neglected it."

Make every effort to shoulder your full share of the responsibility for the salvation and peace of the world. Don't allow unconcern and neglect to contribute to the trend toward spiritual decay any more than you would avoid your material obligations.

A man built a house on the ground without a foundation against which the stream broke, and immediately it fell, and the ruin of that house was great. (Lk. 6:49)

Jesus, keep alive in me a Christian sense of personal responsibility.

If He Only Knew

An architect who had worked for a large corporation for many years was called in one day by the board of directors and given plans for a model house to be built in the most exclusive residential section of the city. The chairman instructed him to spare no expense, to use the finest materials and the best labor available.

As the work progressed, the architect began to think: "No one will ever know what goes into the unseen parts. Why hire such expensive labor? Why use such costly materials?"

He began to substitute inferior materials, to hire inferior labor, pocketing the difference.

Shortly after the house was finished, the chairman of the board held a reception to celebrate its completion. After making a lengthy speech, he amazed the architect by presenting him with the keys to the house.

"We give you this house," he said, "as a token of the high esteem we have for your many years of splendid and faithful service."

Whatever a man sows, that he will also reap. (Gal. 6:7)

Just Judge, help us to remember to sow here what we want to reap hereafter — goodness, truth, justice, peace, beauty, piety.

The Chain of Gratitude

Traffic was light on the parkway when a lady driver felt a sudden tug at the steering wheel. She pulled over and, sure enough, her tire was as flat as could be.

The roads were barren and the unhappy woman was miles from the nearest telephone. As she made ready to resign herself to an unpleasant wait, a lone driver happened along.

He passed her by, stopped and backed up. In a few skillful moments he changed the tire, and then explained why he had done so.

"I'm grateful to be of any help," he said, "because I'm lucky to be alive."

It turned out that he had been rescued after being trapped for hours in a serious fire. Many of his friends had not been so fortunate.

Gratitude can come from many sources. When someone does us an unexpected service, it sparks us to show our thankfulness to God and to others by showing a like concern for our fellow man. See what you can do.

Jesus then took the loaves, and when He had given thanks, He distributed them . . . so also the fish, as much as they wanted. (Jn. 6:11)

Make me a true Christian, Holy Spirit, by filling me with gratitude.

The Tragedy of Loneliness

A 35-year-old woman in Chicago committed suicide.

To one who didn't know her well, she would have seemed to have everything anyone could want out of life: comfort, social position, and the rest. Yet she often complained of the loneliness that had confronted her in childhood and had followed her all through her life.

Shortly before her death she spoke of the emptiness of her existence and referred to her life as a "horrible mess."

Our hearts should go out to people like this. More often than not their whole outlook would have been healthy and normal if someone had showed a bit of interest in them in the name of Christ.

But left alone — trained only to concentrate on self — the qualities God put in them never get a chance to develop. With no proper outlet, stagnation and decay set in: pent-up energy often goes haywire and an "explosion" inevitably is the result.

Many a human tragedy could be averted by a little thoughtful solicitude on the part of some Christian.

Why are you cast down, O my soul, and why are you disquieted within me? Hope in God; for I shall again praise Him, my help and my God. (Ps. 43:5)

God, help me bring the joy of Christ into the lives of the frustrated and depressed.

The Rich Man's 'Gift'

During the Depression a charitable organization which raised funds partly through the sale of scrap received a large box of lead foil. It was weighed and found to be worth exactly $1.80.

One of the workers in smoothing out a piece of the foil was amused to see that it came from the top of a champagne bottle.

She unrolled another piece and saw it was the same. Finally she unrolled every piece in the box and discovered they were all from the same source — the necks of champagne bottles!

The donor of the lead foil probably regarded the gift as a true act of charity. But how often we limit our giving to mere "leftovers." The true spirit of charity involves a personal sacrifice; the greatest gift is a part of ourselves.

I put on righteousness, and it clothed me; . . . I was eyes to the blind, and feet to the lame. I was a father to the poor. (Job 29:14-16)

Lord, teach me to be as generous with others as You are with me.

The Joy and Hope of Easter

Listen to the opening words of an Easter sermon preached by St. John Chrysostom, patriarch of Constantinople, in the fourth century and you'll understand why he is called "Chrysostom" — golden mouthed.

"Let us celebrate this greatest and most shining feast, in which the Lord has risen from the dead.

"Let us celebrate it with joy, and in equal measure with devotion. For the Lord has risen, and together with Him He has raised the whole world. He has risen, because He has broken the bonds of death."

This great Doctor of the Church concludes with a promise of eternal happiness for those who serve God by thought, word and deed on earth.

"May it be granted to each one of us to reach this happiness, through the grace and mercy of Our Lord Jesus Christ, to Whom, with the Father and the Holy Ghost, be there glory and adoration, world without end. Amen."

Imitate the spirit of St. John and the early Christians in bringing the love and truth of the Risen Christ into the market-place.

If then you have been raised with Christ, seek the things that are above, where Christ is, seated at the right hand of God . . . For you have died, and your life is hid with Christ. (Col. 3:1,3)

O Risen Savior, let me recall that You died and rose again for everyone.

Baby Born After Mother's Death

The death of his mother did not prevent a baby boy from being born alive and well.

The 36-year-old mother had been stricken by a heart attack in her New Jersey home. An ambulance was dispatched from a nearby hospital and brought the dead woman to the emergency room.

Minutes later a doctor performed a Caesarean section, which proved successful.

The difference a few minutes can make between life and death is seldom so clearly dramatized. But it points out how a deep regard for the dignity of a human person can bring forth life even in the presence of death.

In the midst of disturbing events, whether at home or on the larger scene, give top priority to the rights of God and of your fellow man, who bears His image.

A hopeful outlook, backed up by hard spadework, can often bring good from evil, success from failure.

If we have died with Christ, we believe that we shall also live with Him. (Rom. 6:8)

Alert us, O Holy Spirit, to the need for prompt action when the occasion calls for it.

Your Amazing Brain

The human brain can store up 10 billion items of information, according to experts.

Scientists claim that each brain cell can retain at least one piece of knowledge.

It would be a practical impossibility for even the greatest genius to exhaust the potential of his brain.

If an individual took in 25 items of information each second he would have to maintain that pace for eight hours a day over a 40-year period to fill his brain.

The enormous potential of the brain is one more breathtaking evidence of the almost limitless capacity with which the Creator has endowed every human being.

Besides being a delicate, intricate storehouse of ideas, the brain has the ability both to assimilate this wealth of information, and to make particular judgments based on Divine truth.

Increase your reverence for God by developing your brain and putting it to constant use in the spread of His truth, goodness, and beauty.

The plans of the diligent lead surely to abundance. (Prov. 21:5)

Thank You, Creator, for endowing me with both an intellect and a will.

Settle for Nothing but the Best

Fur burglars overlooked the most valuable coats in a New Haven, Conn., store and walked off with several cheaper garments.

Whether the thieves planned their robbery this way or not, it's easy to get values mixed up in the hustle and bustle of modern life.

Even those in honest pursuits are constantly tempted to pass up the deep and lasting values in favor of the trivial and tawdry.

To make sure that you are keeping first things first, set aside a few moments daily to check on your thoughts, words, and deeds of the day.

If you do this faithfully and objectively, fundamental principles will not become obscured or slip into secondary importance.

Above all else be conscious that you are on a pilgrimage. By keeping your sights on eternal treasures, you will not be likely to settle for the fleeting, the valueless.

Do not seek what you are to eat and what you are to drink, nor be of anxious mind . . . your Father knows that you need them. Instead, seek His kingdom, and these things shall be yours as well. (Lk. 12:29-31)

Let not the distractions of this life, O my God, blind me to the never-ending joys of Your kingdom.

Win People, Not Arguments

A businessman left a very important conference after engaging for more than an hour in a heated debate over policy.

As he entered his own office, he muttered in a boastful tone to his secretary, "Well, I guess I won that argument!"

Personal triumph seems to have been the source of this man's happiness.

He seems to have been less interested in helping others than in pushing himself. His was the shallow "pride of being right," not the joy of helping others better to understand the truth.

The true Christian is far less interested in winning a debate, in forcing someone to admit defeat, than in helping them to arrive at the truth.

One seldom wins persons by argument, but always by love.

Death and life are in the power of the tongue. (Prov. 18:21)

Lord, take from me the "pride of being right," and give me the love of sharing with others.

Under His Feet

A homesteader in Texas, suffering financial difficulties, came to the conclusion that he ought to move on to California, where he "could really make some money." He had difficulty getting rid of his property and finally sold it for a very small sum.

Shortly after taking over, the new tenant discovered oil on his land. Within a few short months he became a millionaire.

The farmer had been looking far away for assistance. Yet all the time the solution to all his financial problems lay right under his feet.

Sometimes our very familiarity with the things around us blinds us to their real worth. We think to find our opportunities to do things for God, for example, in some unusual position where we can do extraordinary things. Yet all the while in the humdrum of our daily tasks we have all the opportunities we need to start bringing the love of God to our fellow men.

Unless you see signs and wonders you will not believe. (Jn. 4:48)

Lord, help me to see my opportunities to start reaching for the world in my everyday tasks.

Highlight Youthful Idealism

A quick-thinking 10-year-old boy saved the life of a nine-year-old girl who had fallen through the ice on a river near Toledo, Ohio.

Spotting Janet Rospert struggling in the cold waters of the ice-crusted river, young Richard Dicken wasted no time in putting his ax to the best use he ever made of it.

He quickly climbed a nearby tree and chopped off a sturdy branch. Then, hurrying to the shore, he reached out with the branch to Janet, who was precariously hanging onto a thin piece of ice. In a matter of moments he had pulled her to safety.

In these days much is said and written about the violence perpetrated by youngsters. But there are countless instances like this that reflect the idealism instilled by God in every boy and girl.

Do something to highlight the good accomplished by the majority of young people and you may go far in popularizing a new and nobler trend among all young people.

Rejoice . . . in your youth, and let your heart cheer you . . . walk in the ways of your heart and the sight of your eyes. (Ecc. 11:9)

O Lord, help me to focus attention on youth's potential for good rather than on their shortcomings.

Make It Your Personal Business

There's no substitute for you. That particularly applies to the part you should play in any organization to which you belong.

What you do — or fail to do — will strengthen or weaken your organization just that much.

You have a vocation from Almighty God to make your personal contribution to human affairs. Make it your business therefore to:

■ Encourage capable leaders to run for office. Back them when they are elected.

■ Insist on the secret ballot for all elections and important issues.

■ See that delegates are chosen according to fair and honest processes.

■ Keep the organization alive by making meetings more meaningful and giving listless members a reason for participating in the activities of the organization.

Fight the good fight of the faith. (1 Tim. 6:12)

Keep me mindful, O Lord, of my obligation to every organization of which I am a member.

A Passion for Gold

Reviewing two books on the California gold rush, Time magazine commented:

"Together they give an unforgettable impression of a mighty movement of people, unorganized and yet queerly efficient, undisciplined and yet tenacious, unbeatable, ignorant, misled, unprepared, unaided, persisting despite almost every obstacle."

This tremendous movement of people from all over the nation to the West is one of the most stirring passages in all our history.

Yet the driving purpose behind this "push" was a passion for gold.

If only those who already possess gold — "the treasure of truth" — would strive as vigorously to share their treasure with the world, what a difference it would make in every phase of our life today!

> **I count everything as loss because of the surpassing worth of knowing Christ Jesus my Lord. For His sake I . . . count them as refuse, in order that I may gain Christ. (Phil. 3:8)**

> *Lord, give me the loving wisdom that will enable me to bring You to others even as I reject the passing treasures of the here and now.*

Overemphasis on Self

Parents and teachers are so preoccupied with protecting the young that they overemphasize self-preservation, self-sanctification, self-development, and self-enjoyment. Without meaning any harm, they often give children the impression they have but one mission in life — to take care of themselves. They seldom stress their obligation to the common good of all — to "love thy neighbor as thyself."

Of course, as Thomas Aquinas said: "A man must have a certain anxiety about the acquisition or preservation of external things."

Everyone should have a reasonable interest in nutritious food, proper clothing, good housing, and other necessities and comforts. But many so overemphasize their own interests that they seldom devote time and energy to provide the urgently needed personal leadership to win for the great masses of mankind the bare necessities of life which God intends as their minimum right.

Care of self is most important, but is only part of Christianity. By failing to pass on the fullness of Christ's message, many are fencing their children in, robbing them of the more abundant life God meant them to have.

Do not be conformed to this world but be transformed by the renewal of your mind. (Rom. 12:2)

O Lord, broaden my vision to include others in my solicitude for an eternal reward of joy.

To Relax, Try Knitting

Knitting is one of the best possible tranquilizers, claims a London doctor.

In recommending that men as well as women get a set of knitting needles and start making a sweater for themselves, he said: "The sense of creating a garment or a piece of fabric from its basic elements is very satisfying."

Any practical steps that help individuals to stir up their creative power should be encouraged.

But no matter how small the beginnings may be, care should be taken to set one's ultimate sights on big and worthwhile goals.

Those who are on the lookout for ways and means to be of service to others are seldom in need of tranquilizers.

Seek to discover and harness the bit of greatness entrusted to you by God and use it to benefit others.

You will find such effort far more challenging and satisfying than if you merely try to keep yourself occupied.

This commandment we have from Him, that he who loves God should love his brother also. (1 Jn. 4:21)

Let me find my peace, O Lord, in showing love to others for Your sake.

Time Will Tell

People who strive to do great things for God and men have no difficulty in using their time. Usually their only difficulty is to find enough time to squeeze in all the things they want to do.

The same holds true of those who hate God and who seek to enslave men. Driven on by a purpose, evil though it is, they regard all time as precious. They spend as much of it as possible on their cause, as little as necessary on themselves.

Those with no cause beyond self often find time hanging on their hands and try to think of ways of "killing time." Yes, the saying, "Tell me what you do with your time and I'll tell you what you are," has a lot of truth in it.

In a poem, "God's Minute," someone once wrote:

I have only just a minute,
Only sixty seconds in it,
Forced upon me, can't refuse it,
Didn't seek it, didn't choose it,
But it's up to me to use it,
I must suffer if I lose it,
Give account if I abuse it,
Just a tiny minute —
But Eternity is in it.

Now is the acceptable time . . . the day of salvation. (2 Cor. 6:2)

O God, keep me aware that You will require me one day to give an account of my time.

Wider Horizons Through Books

"Reading maketh a full man." These words of the English essayist Francis Bacon are engraved on the walls of the Library of Congress.

Many go through a lifetime depriving themselves of the happiness that comes with development of their intellectual and spiritual powers.

Yet it is within the power of every individual to open the doors that will lead to a more meaningful and purposeful existence. One door to which everyone has a key is the habit of good reading.

If you devote only 15 minutes each day to a good book, you are bound to widen your horizons.

A constant and almost endless variety of books awaits you in many libraries. The literary treasures on their shelves are yours for the asking.

Good reading, whether novels, history, biography, or spiritual works, will help you develop the talent entrusted to you by the Lord.

You will thus be equipped to play a more effective role in shaping modern trends toward God instead of away from Him.

Happy is the man who finds wisdom, and . . . gets understanding. (Prov. 3:13)

Thanks to You, O Spirit of Wisdom, for providing me with the means of leading a worthwhile life.

Do It by Doing It

A popular novelist was asked to talk at a large Eastern university to a group of the undergraduates. Those present all had literary ambitions.

"How many of you really want to be writers?" the famous author began.

Every student in the room raised his hand.

"In that case," said the novelist, "there's no point in wasting your time here. Go home and write."

This may have been a little brusque, but there is a point to what he said. If you want to do anything, you have to start doing it. If you want to cook, you have to get into the kitchen. If you want to swim, you have to get into the water.

In working for God, for one's fellow man, or for oneself, we cannot expect to do great things until we've at least made a start. Take a step on your own towards Christ, and He will help you the rest of the way.

We must work the works of Him who sent Me, while it is day; night comes, when no one can work. (Jn. 9:4)

Jesus, help me to realize that the smallest action is more important than the biggest intention.

It's Easy to Tell Others

A man who wrote a book called "Living Without Liquor," blamed most of his troubles on alcohol when arrested in Boston. He had tried to cash three worthless checks after being fired from a dishwasher's job.

The 49-year-old man held a graduate degree from a leading university. When the judge asked him how he happened to wind up washing dishes after "all that college education," the frustrated man summed it all up in one word: "Liquor."

He admitted he would have been better off if he had practiced the recommendations he made to others in his book.

It's easy to slip into the habit of preaching one thing and practicing another.

Most of us can wax strong on what should be done, for instance, to improve politics, education, or literature and yet not do anything toward a positive solution ourselves.

Strive to translate your noble ideas into concrete application.

Not everyone who says to Me, "Lord, Lord," shall enter the kingdom of heaven, but he who does the will of My Father who is in heaven. (Mt. 7:21)

Give me the wisdom and strength, O Lord, to practice what I preach.

Child Keeps Family Together

A lesson in keeping a family together was taught by a 10-year-old girl in Atlanta.

Six children were found living in a tiny apartment. The father had disappeared and the mother was hospitalized.

Sally, the oldest child, had taken things into her own hands. She got her brother, seven, and sister, five, off to school every morning and then left the three youngest with neighbors.

After school she would rush home to pick up the youngsters and get the housework done.

When city officials told Sally that children were not allowed to care for themselves, she pleaded: "Please don't separate us! We belong together. We want to stay together."

It is often a crisis that unleashes the capabilities that God has instilled in young and old alike. This tremendous potential, still untouched by most, is hopeful proof that humanity can always rise to new heights despite our shortcomings.

The Lord is the everlasting God, the Creator . . . He gives power to the faint, and to him who has no might He increases strength. (Is. 40:28,29)

Help me, O Holy Spirit, to put to good use the power You have entrusted to me.

Save Yourself the Trouble

A smuggler in Korea found that his questionable activities led him into a vicious circle of trouble.

When jailed for not being able to pay a $13,450 fine for smuggling, officials discovered that this fine was incurred in an attempt to pay off a previous $37,118 fine for smuggling.

Trying to cover up mistakes or to correct mischievous blunders usually creates more trouble than playing the game straight in the first place, as God expects each of us to do.

So rather than wear yourself out on the frustrating treadmill of merely avoiding evil, make it your business to concentrate on doing good.

By following a positive pattern in all you think, say, and do, you will relieve yourself of the dull, gnawing nuisance of negative living.

Better still, you will have something worthwhile to show for your life when you have to make your final report to the Lord of heaven and earth.

Let us not grow weary in well-doing, for in due season we shall reap, if we do not lose heart. (Gal. 6:9)

Grant, O Jesus, that I may be so busy doing good that I will have neither the time nor the inclination for evil.

The Security That Lasts

An insurance advertisement listed the following among the "many perils" that endanger the security of your home, possessions and savings:

"Fire . . . windstorm . . . explosion . . . burglary and robbery . . . personal injury . . . property damage . . . lightning . . . aircraft damage . . . damage by fall of trees . . . riot and strike damage . . . malicious mischief . . . vandalism . . . collapse of dwelling . . . water damage from plumbing or heating systems . . ."

A momentary reflection on such threats and hazards is a forceful reminder that material possessions do not bring the enduring security for which the human spirit yearns.

Show a reasonable concern in protecting the physical necessities and comforts of life. But take care at the same time not to make them the "be all" and "end all" of your existence.

Because you are made in God's image, nothing short of Him will ever satisfy you. Ponder from time to time this profound, sensible advice of the Master:

You cannot serve God and mammon. (Mt. 6:24)

Keep my sights set on the treasures that last forever, O Lord.

Locked in a Refrigerated Truck

A driver became a prisoner in his own refrigerated truck while delivering meat to a restaurant in New York.

After double-parking his truck, he hopped inside to get his order. But the door clicked shut behind him.

For the next four hours he banged on the insulated walls, stamped on the cold wet floor and shouted himself hoarse. No one either heard him or missed him or the meat delivery. He didn't even get a ticket for blocking traffic. He simply shivered and waited.

In the middle of the afternoon the chef asked about his order. The manager, noticing the truck outside the restaurant, went out and opened the big refrigerator door. Out staggered a chilled but grateful driver, none the worse for wear.

Slight mistakes can be dangerous, even disastrous. God expects you to be ever alert in doing what is right and just. You will accomplish much good and avoid considerable trouble if you do.

Hold fast what is good, abstain from every form of evil. (1 Th. 5:21-22)

Guard me against despair at my own imperfections, O Lord, and against judgmentalism at others' imperfections.

Be Reasonable About It

May 4

During a cold spell in Georgia a radio station urged people several times to turn down their thermostats five degrees in order to conserve the supply of natural gas.

After the station had repeated the request several times, one overcautious man phoned in this unexpected complaint:

"I've been turning down the thermostat five degrees every time you asked, and it's now 40 degrees in the living room and I'm getting tired of it."

If this well-meaning gentleman had considered the spirit rather than the letter of the radio plea, he might have had a warmer time of it.

God has revealed certain specific and immutable laws through His own divine broadcasting system to guide us safely through this life to the endless joys of heaven.

But He expects each of us to show good sense in observing them.

Christ warned all of us to fulfill the spirit as well as the letter of the law.

Hear, O Israel, the commandments of life; listen and learn wisdom! (Bar. 3:9)

Help us to honor You from our heart, not merely with our lips, Father.

Which Direction?

In an English churchyard the following epitaph is carved on one of the ancient headstones:

"Remember, man that passeth by,
As thou art now, so once was I;
And as I am so thou must be;
Prepare thyself to follow me."

Some visitor with a sense of discrimination scribbled the following underneath:

"To follow thee's not my intent,
— Unless I know which way thou went."

It's easy to wander through life aimlessly, seldom giving any thought to the fact that the ultimate destination for each of us is either heaven or hell.

Where each of us goes depends on where we want to go.

On what we do, or fail to do, over a lifetime for the love of God and others, as well as for ourselves, depends our eternal destination.

Be faithful unto death, and I will give you the crown of life. (Rev. 1:10)

Master, may we be ever conscious of our eternal destiny.

Before the Verdict, Prayer

In a murder trial in Colorado the jury gave the nation a stirring example of its sense of responsibility. When the trial was over, the foreman of the 12-man panel announced that before reaching a verdict the group had said this prayer:

"Almighty God, help us in this hour of deliberation. Give us wisdom that we may be guided to a just and fair verdict to all concerned. Let Thy spirit descend upon us so that our conscience will become Thy will.

"With malice towards none and forethought of the duty we are about to perform, let us, Thy mortals, have divine guidance in this deliberation. Amen."

This is a heartening sign. When more people in positions of responsibility show publicly their dependence upon God, there cannot help but be a great change for the better.

Give Your servant therefore an understanding mind . . . that I may discern between good and evil. (1 Kg. 3:9)

Spirit of Wisdom, guide our actions and those of people in positions of authority.

Far From Wasted

A reporter called on Thomas A. Edison one afternoon to interview him about a substitute for lead in the manufacture of storage batteries that the scientist was seeking. Edison informed the man he had made 20,000 experiments but none of them had worked.

"But aren't you discouraged by all this waste of effort?" the reporter asked, amazed.

"Waste!" exclaimed Mr. Edison. "There's nothing wasted. I have discovered 20,000 things that won't work."

From time to time we may feel that some good action of ours has not born fruit. But we should not be discouraged: easy success is more likely to harm us than gradual achievement. And often an action that may seem in vain can have a delayed, important effect, like a seed ripening into grain.

> **As for (the seed that) was sown on good soil, this is he who hears the word and understands it; he indeed bears fruit, and yields . . . a hundredfold. (Mt. 13:23)**

Lord of the harvest, give us the grace to persevere.

It Takes Time

Once I watched some children plant seeds in a garden. I saw the careful attention with which they watered them.

The next morning, the children rushed to the window, expecting to see the garden filled with blooms. In their disappointment and impatience they proceeded to neglect the garden and finally the seeds died without ever having produced anything.

This simple experience can be an example to all not to be impatient of results. The true bearer of Christ does not expect his good work to bear immediate fruit. He does not expect to plant a seed and get a rosebush overnight.

Indeed, he may labor at length and apparently in vain. But the truth is that he is winning all the time, because it is the labor itself that counts. As Paul said:

> **I planted, Apollos watered, but God gave the growth. So neither he who plants nor he who waters is anything, but only God who gives the growth. (1 Cor. 3:6-7)**

Lord, help me to combine in myself good will, courage and patience.

Just as Easy

A child who had spent quite a bit of extra time at her prayers one evening, and had been questioned by her mother as to the reason, replied: "I was praying that all bad people would be good and all good people nice!"

One of the greatest injuries to religion comes from a few of its most loyal adherents who are correct in all matters save one. They persist in being disagreeable when it would be just as easy to remain agreeable, even while differing with others.

If they realized how that slightly sour note has a big effect in keeping large numbers away from religion, many would undoubtedly change to a more pleasant attitude without delay.

It is most important for a Christopher to be pleasantly firm when it is necessary to be firm. But being disagreeable is a sign of weakness.

He who says he is in the light and hates his brother is in the darkness still. He who loves his brother abides in the light, and in it there is no cause for stumbling. (1 Jn. 2:9-10)

Lord, help me to reflect your kindness to me in my dealings with others.

What Damage One Rodent Can Do

One little rat caused a dike to collapse in England.

After the rodent had burrowed through the embankment of a canal, water began seeping through. Slowly but surely the original trickle became a sizable stream. Soon one bank collapsed and a 40-foot breakthrough let the water pour out in torrents.

Three million gallons of water escaped; the canal was drained for seven miles; more than one million fish were swept away and a 20-foot gorge was channeled through a nearby field.

It took 60 men with bulldozers three weeks to shift 30,000 tons of soil and repair the damages.

As one rodent caused tremendous harm, so can one individual like you start a chain reaction that will benefit everyone.

You may never be aware of the far-reaching good resulting from a seemingly insignificant prayer, word, or deed. But God is, and that is what counts.

In everything God works for good with those who love Him, who are called according to His purpose. (Rom. 8:28)

Inspire me to see in the smallest details an opportunity to honor You, God.

One Mistake Stalls Train

Ever hear of a passenger train running out of fuel? It happened on the run from Oklahoma City to St. Louis some time ago.

When the express ground to a dead stop 12 miles outside of Springfield, Mo., the embarrassed crew had to admit to all the passengers that the supply of fuel for the diesel engines was exhausted.

There was nothing to do but wait until a fuel truck could be dispatched from Springfield.

An inquiry revealed that all the trouble stemmed from one employee's failure to fill the train's fuel tanks in Oklahoma City.

Trouble involving a few hundred persons or even millions can so often be traced back to the oversight or neglect of one individual.

There's a hopeful side to the picture. Just as one person can cause far-reaching harm by a single act of omission, so can that same individual benefit countless people by living up to his obligations both to God and man.

We put no obstacles in any one's way so that no fault may be found with our ministry. (2 Cor. 6:3)

Help me, Master, to prove by my deeds that I am concerned about the rights of others.

A Life Saved

Thirty-six-year-old Juan Garcia decided to end it all by throwing himself in front of a truck in Valencia, Spain. The driver swerved into a wall to avoid the would-be suicide.

Infuriated, he starting running after Garcia, who leaped in front of another oncoming truck. The second driver swiftly turned his truck to the side of the road. Before he could stop, however, it rolled down an embankment.

With two truck drivers hot on his trail, Garcia leaped on a horse conveniently standing by, and galloped to a nearby railroad bridge. He tied a rope around his neck and suspended himself from a girder. Laborers who saw him dangling rescued him in the nick of time.

Garcia was jailed by police for disturbing the peace and causing damage to two trucks.

This is an extraordinary case to be sure. But there will always be hope for the world when most people try to save life rather than destroy it.

Do what you can to make everyone aware that every human being counts because they are made in God's image and likeness.

God created man in His own image ... male and female He created them. (Gen. 1:27)

Thank You, Creator, for forming us in Your divine image.

Women at Their Best

Women are more careful with keys than men are, according to a Canadian locksmith with 23 years' experience.

He claims that "men break keys, lose them, or get impatient and jam them into locks," while "women take better care of locks because they symbolize security."

Women render an important service by guarding the security and stability of the home.

But the world beyond the home also needs the noble qualities with which God has blessed them — peace, justice, decency, culture, and an innate spiritual sense.

Every woman, therefore, has it within her power to help renew and refresh the face of the earth.

It takes vision and courage, to be sure, to rise above the inclination to confine these attributes to her immediate surroundings.

But by projecting them into the heart of a world, now withering and dying without them, women can go far in contributing to the peace of mankind.

Open your mouth for the dumb, for the rights of all who are left desolate . . . judge righteously, maintain the rights of the poor and needy. (Prov. 31:8-9)

Son of Mary, bless all women who strive to renew the face of the earth.

A Generous Plumber

A Detroit plumber was the first man on record to decline the $8 a day recompense for jury duty.

Although he took 20 days away from his own work to serve, he frankly admitted that it involved no special hardship for him.

"Accepting pay which I don't need for jury duty would be like getting paid for voting," was the comment he made.

Few can afford to pass up the token payment given to those called as jurors. The majority who serve must sacrifice their means of livelihood for the period of their service.

Still, it is refreshing to know that even one person would take such a generous attitude while playing his part to protect the processes of free government.

God bless the generous, especially those who make a personal sacrifice to apply His divine law and order to the running of human affairs.

You received without paying, give without pay. (Mt. 10:8)

Fill me with a generous spirit, Jesus.

Stumped by a Safe

A safe got the better of a burglar in a Kentucky store. The evidence left behind by the thief revealed his ignominious defeat.

When the owner arrived at the scene of the crime the next morning, he found the floor littered with broken chisels, bent screw drivers, and pinch bars. Despite a thorough battering, the sturdy safe stood unbroken in its usual spot.

The burglar had to settle for slim pickings for his night of hard work — $20 from the cash register and 12 cartons of cigarettes.

Some individuals spend a whole lifetime using every available tool trying to shatter immutable truth. But no one ever succeeds.

Show by your life that you earnestly desire to comply and cooperate with divine truth — never defy it.

By so doing you will not only have tranquility in your own heart and soul, but you will radiate it into the lives of countless others.

Keep the law and the commandments, and be merciful and just, so that it may be well with you . . . consider what almsgiving accomplishes and how righteousness delivers. (Tob. 14:9,11)

Author of truth, help us to walk in Your truth and to be holy in Your sight all the days of our lives.

Good Intentions Not Enough

Four teenagers met sudden death in New Jersey when their speeding car crashed into a tree after skidding for 216 feet.

Six months before the fatal wreck, the 17-year-old driver had his license temporarily suspended for reckless driving.

The dead boy's father had been reluctant to allow him to drive again as a minor. But the boy promised never to speed again, saying: "Dad, do you think I'm a fool? I've just lost my license for three months. It's not going to happen again."

But good intentions are of little avail unless backed up by a firm determination to translate noble theories into actual practice.

Life is too short to take foolish risks involving the temporal and eternal destiny of others as well as yourself.

Remember that much more than wishful thinking and empty promises must distinguish your stay on earth.

This night your soul is required of you; and the things you have prepared, whose will they be? (Lk. 12:20)

Help me prove my love for You, Savior.

Making the Most of Life

"Content makes poor men rich; discontent makes rich men poor," was Benjamin Franklin's way of expressing the important role that satisfaction plays in the lives of one and all without exception.

But many people needlessly lead dissatisfied lives. They don't realize that the Lord has given each of them the basic ingredients for a happy, full existence.

The very meaning of the word "satisfaction" is derived from two Latin words: "satis" meaning "enough" and "facere" meaning "to do" or "to make."

Only those who "do enough" or "make enough" of their lives, therefore, enjoy that peace and contentment for which every human being strives.

Be sure to be a "doer" to "make enough" of your life. Develop and put to good use whatever talents the Lord has loaned you. You will experience the joy of living completely and avoid the boredom of half living if you do.

We must work the works of Him who sent Me, while it is day; night comes, when no one can work. (Jn. 9:4)

Deepen in me, Divine Master, a determination to make the most of the years of my life.

Saving Lives Was His Specialty

A skipper who saved 106 lives during his 50 years at sea was awarded a gold medal for meritorious service.

Capt. George H. Grant's rescues included two men on a sinking fishing boat in the Gulf Stream, three others on a raft off the west coast of Mexico, 17 sailors from a naval vessel that sank outside of San Francisco harbor, as well as 83 survivors of a collision between a tanker and an icebreaker.

The most unique rescue involved one of his own sailors who fell overboard and was not missed until several hours later. The captain immediately turned his ship about and retraced the exact course. After a careful search the seaman was eventually picked up unharmed.

You may not be able to go to sea and duplicate such rescues, but during your voyage through life, you have countless opportunities to help your fellows by showing a Christ-like concern and alertness for those in distress.

There is no fear in love, but perfect love casts out fear. (1 Jn. 4:18)

Help me, O Lord, to be ever on the lookout for those in trouble.

More Than Weapons Needed for Peace

Those who believe that the survival of our country depends on having "the biggest bang, the best weapons system, or a lot of money" were reminded by Admiral Arleigh Burke a few years ago that much more than these are needed.

The Chief of Naval Operations, speaking at a graduation ceremony at Annapolis told the midshipmen:

"Without sound moral and spiritual values, firmly rooted in the character of our people, our instruments become merely weapons of suicide . . . We achieve nothing if we seek only material power."

Each of us can make a personal contribution to lasting peace by protecting the spiritual roots of our nation.

In these hectic times it is easy to put too much faith in material values and weapons systems, and too little in the enduring ones of the spirit.

Unless the Lord watches over the city, the watchman stays awake in vain. (Ps. 127:1)

Remind me, and help me remind others, Holy Spirit, that God is the Author of our liberty.

Living Better While Living Longer

Mozart died at the age of 35, Alexander the Great at 33, Shelley at 30, and Keats at 26.

Because of the great strides made by scientists, doctors, and pharmacists, the average person today can expect to live years longer than those who lived even half a century ago.

The medical profession has made an outstanding contribution to mankind by helping countless millions to live longer and healthier lives.

Take advantage of this extra time by adding meaning and purpose to your comparatively short stay on earth.

It is a precious opportunity to rise above self-centered interests and reach for the great spiritual fulfillment which is the very reason for your existence.

God made you to know, love, and serve Him in this life so that you may be happy with Him forever in the next.

The longest life is all too short to prepare adequately for that eternal reward. Make it a point, therefore, to live better while living longer.

None of us lives to himself, and none of us dies to himself. If we live, we live to the Lord, and if we die, we die to the Lord; so, then, whether we live or . . . die, we are the Lord's. (Rom. 14:7-8)

I thank You, Father, for creating me for Yourself, now and for all eternity.

Hidden Power

A 65-year-old man risked his life to rescue a teenage girl who had jumped from a subway platform in London.

Although he heard a train approaching, the elderly man didn't hesitate a moment to leap down onto the tracks and try to prevent the 18-year-old girl from killing herself.

Meanwhile, the engineer of the oncoming train saw what was happening and quickly applied his emergency brakes. He brought the cars to a stop only a few yards from the hysterical girl and her rescuer.

Few people realize what great capabilities they possess until an emergency arises. Then they often surprise themselves by the way they rise to the occasion.

Don't wait for the unusual or extreme to bring out the power that God has put in your keeping.

The contribution that you personally can make by being resourceful and courageous is much needed in today's topsy-turvy world.

> **Why, one will hardly die for a righteous man — though perhaps for a good man one will dare even to die. But . . . while we were yet sinners Christ died for us. (Rom. 5:7-8)**

Inspire me, O Holy Spirit, to put to good use the talents You have entrusted to me.

They Work for You

Three painters in Milwaukee parked their cars in a two-hour zone and attached the following note to their windshields: "Painters working inside."

Upon returning each worker found a parking ticket on his car, together with this response: "Policemen working outside."

Many motorists wish that traffic police would be a little less vigilant. This in itself is at least an unwitting tribute to the fact that these public servants are doing their jobs efficiently.

One hears much these days about the few in government — local, state, or national — who are lax or corrupt. But too little is said about the far greater number who devotedly and conscientiously serve their country year in and year out.

You can contribute to better government by giving your moral support to worthy rank-and-file government workers. They do not seek special notice or privilege. But they do need and deserve your confidence and assurance.

The memory of the righteous is a blessing. (Prov. 10:7)

Bless, O Lord, those who strive to serve You and country year in and year out.

Perseverance

Prizes for perfect attendance records went begging at two meetings.

At the annual banquet of a club in Midland, Tex., the president announced special citations for members who had faithfully come to every meeting. But when he read off the names of the winners, the first five were conspicuous by their absence.

In Sherringham, England, high-school officials were similarly embarrassed. A teenager failed to put in an appearance at a special ceremony at which he was to be given a prize for perfect attendance during the previous school term.

Many who show bright promise in doggedly pursuing a worthy goal, often succumb to the fatal mistake of taking it easy on the home stretch.

No matter how steadfast you may have been in the past, and no matter how much devotion you may have shown to high ideals, make sure you do not falter or fall before you render the final accounting of your life to the Supreme Judge.

Who endures to the end will be saved. (Mt. 10:22)

Protect and strengthen me, O Jesus, especially when I feel like giving up.

True Wisdom

Solomon, King of Israel, began his reign as a teenager of 18 about a thousand years before Christ. He ruled for 40 years and was distinguished for his wisdom.

When he ascended the throne as a young king, he did not ask for riches and a long life. Instead, he beseeched the Lord to give him an understanding heart so that he might rule his people wisely and justly.

God was pleased with his request, and many, including the Queen of Sheba, came from afar to seek his advice. Solomon was known as the wisest of men.

God also blessed Solomon with worldly riches and honors. And Solomon built the temple in Jerusalem.

None among us are given the unusual advantages entrusted to Solomon. But each of us has some ability, however small, to be God's instrument in restoring wisdom and justice to God's world.

> **Give Your servant therefore an understanding mind to govern Your people, that I may discern between good and evil. (1 Kg. 3:9)**

> *God, grant that I may speak with judgment and have thoughts worthy of what I have received.*

Peace of Mind Can't Be Bought

Police tried to dissuade a New Jersey motorist from scattering $50 bills along the highway.

Their efforts to make him return to his parked Cadillac were unsuccessful. His only comment was: "I don't want the car or money. All I want is peace of mind."

Few people get so sick of money that they toss away $50 bills. But most who achieve pocketbook success miss the real joy of living.

Material possessions are certainly necessary, but we are composed of soul as well as body. We throw our lives off balance if we concentrate on material things and neglect due attention to our mind, heart, and soul.

You are made for heaven. Nothing short of it will ever satisfy you. Keep that goal uppermost in your life and you will always have peace of mind, no matter how small or large your share of earthly goods may be.

Man shall not live by bread alone but by every word that proceeds from the mouth of God. (Mt. 4:4)

Thank You, Spirit of Wisdom, for the contentment and joy that come from You alone.

Anger Destroys a House

An exasperated man got the worst of it when he lost his temper and set fire to his cat.

While filling his cigarette lighter some of the fluid dripped on his hands as well as on the cat which was brushing against his leg.

When he tested the lighter, the fluid on his hands ignited and in a burst of anger he threw the burning lighter at the cat.

The flaming animal took off in a mad dash about the house, setting fire to all it touched. The owner couldn't catch up with the running torch or extinguish the many fires.

As a result his house burned to the ground and he was sentenced to 75 days in jail for cruelty to animals.

Anger often causes damaging chain reactions which harm many and help no one.

With the aid of God's grace direct your pent-up energy into constructive channels. It is the hallmark of a mature human being.

The vexation of a fool is known at once, but the prudent man ignores an insult. (Prov. 12:16)

Teach me, Gentle Shepherd, to disagree without being disagreeable.

The Time Is Now

A meeting of the board of directors was going on in hell. Satan was greatly concerned over the fact that business was not increasing with the speed that he had anticipated. He wanted to reach as many people as possible and draw them into hell.

One man jumped up and said: "I'll go back to earth and convince people that there is no heaven."

"That won't do," said Satan. "We've tried it before and it doesn't work."

"I'll convince them that there is no hell," offered a second man.

"No — that doesn't work either," said Satan.

A wise old veteran in the back of the room rose and said: "If you let me go back to earth I can fill this place. I'll just convince them that there is no hurry."

So often we are inclined to put off until tomorrow what we should do today. We do this because we figure there is no hurry. But there is a hurry about saving our souls and those of others. Tomorrow may be too late!

We must work the works of Him who sent Me while it is day; night comes, when no one can work. As long as I am in the world, I am the light of the world. (Jn. 9:4-5)

Father of all, give me the strength to start right now to work for the coming of Your Kingdom in all hearts by the testimony of my life.

Freedom Begins With You

"None can love freedom heartily but good men," said the poet John Milton, "the rest love not freedom, but license."

On the sharp difference between freedom and license most people will agree. But it is not easy for the average citizen to convince himself that he personally strengthens or weakens free government by his actions.

So much depends on how each citizen exerts or fails to exert his intelligent, conscientious and patriotic influence. These thoughts may help:

■ The total population of town, city, state and nation is nothing more than a multiplication of you.

■ To be an enlightened citizen you must be familiar with the nature and functions of your government.

■ To exert a force for good you must take an interest in government that is better than hit-and-miss.

Do more than pay lip service to "God Bless America." Prove your sincerity by your deeds.

He who is not with Me is against Me. (Mt. 12:30)

Thank You, Heavenly Father, for a share in Your divine freedom.

Four-Leaf Clovers by the Thousands

Collecting four-leaf clovers was quite a hobby for a mother and her 17-year-old daughter in British Columbia.

When asked what they intended to do with the 3,425 four-leaf clovers which they kept between the pages of a phone book, the mother replied: "We do not plan to do anything special with them. I guess we'll just keep on collecting them."

A hobby can be a pleasant diversion and need not have any special aim so long as it remains incidental to everything else.

But there is even greater value in having a hobby which benefits others as well as yourself. Most people are seeking fulfillment as well as relaxation.

Devote some of your spare time and energy to the sick, the poor, the aged; offer your services to youth groups as well as educational and political organizations.

If you do, you will find an ever-broadening outlet for the abilities entrusted to you by God.

Bear one another's burdens, and so fulfill the law of Christ. (Gal. 6:2)

Help me, my Maker, to lead a purpose-filled life.

Promote Respect for Learning

Daniel Webster reminds us:

"If we work upon marble, it will perish.

"If we work upon brass, time will efface it.

"If we rear temples, they will crumble to dust.

"But if we work upon men's immortal minds, if we imbue them with high principles, with the just fear of God and love of their fellow man, we engrave on those tablets something which no time can efface, and which will brighten and brighten to all eternity."

Any nation that places more emphasis on the material than on the spiritual is trifling with disaster.

Put the values of the mind and spirit before all else. Develop a respect for true learning among young people.

Don't let youth become satisfied with mere information. Encourage intelligent thinking and sound judgment. Help boys and girls acquire the complete, well-rounded development that will have effects for time and for eternity.

> **If riches are a desirable possession in life, what is richer than wisdom who effects all things? (Wis. of Sol. 8:5)**

> *Deepen in youth, O Lord, a love of that wisdom which endures.*

Missing: One House

Officials in Detroit had good reason to be embarrassed when they received an indignant phone call from a lady who demanded:

"What happened? I had a seven-room house. Now all I've got is a vacant lot with an elm tree."

A quick investigation revealed that the irate woman certainly had good reason to complain. A wrecking crew had used their bulldozer on one house too many while clearing an area for factory sites.

In today's fast-moving world action is often mistaken for progress. But sound thinking must precede action if human beings are to be helped, not hurt. Standards of love, truth, and justice must be respected, not overlooked or flaunted.

See to it that everyone's basic spiritual and material rights are given due consideration. By doing so you will be making a valuable contribution to true and lasting progress in our world.

It is not good for a man to be without knowledge, and he who makes haste with his feet misses his way. (Prov. 19:2)

Give us the wisdom, Holy Spirit, to seek true progress, not deceptive imitations of it.

The High Price of Ambition

"Where ambition ends happiness begins," runs an old Hungarian proverb.

Persons driven by an inordinate ambition to "get ahead" — whether it is to be the richest man on the block, the best dressed girl in the class or the wittiest person at the party — usually become so involved in selling their own wares that they have no time for normal peace of heart, mind and soul.

Such limitless zeal for limited goals spells only the deprival of even the "A, B, C's" of happiness.

Shakespeare's oft-repeated plea from "Henry VIII" merits more than passing reflection:

"I charge thee, fling away ambition.
By that sin fell the angels; how can man then
The image of his Maker, hope to win by it?"

But there is an ambition that brings true joy, though it usually goes by a different name. It is the unquenchable desire to serve — to be of service to God and to others for His sake.

Make that noble goal the object of your thought and action.

Earnestly desire the higher gifts. (1 Cor. 12:31)

O Lord our God, help us to find our joy in serving others for Your sake.

The Pull of the Sea

A 10-year-old suburban youngster had such a longing to go to sea that he couldn't resist making a preliminary try on a swampy lake in his neighborhood.

One day he found a piece of driftwood, which he used as a trial ship for his maiden voyage.

All went well at first, but he soon discovered that he could not control his makeshift vessel. Darkness set in and he was drifting far from shore.

Passers-by heard the boy's cries and summoned police. They were not equipped to cope with amateur seafarers, especially in swampy waters. After many vain attempts at rescue, one policeman finally reached the boy by wading through water up to his chin.

Christ encourages all of us to "launch out into the deep." But He expects us to be daring without being reckless.

Encourage rather than stifle the spirit of venture in young people by directing it into worthwhile channels.

The hour is coming when all who are in the tombs . . . will come forth, those who have done good, to the resurrection of life. (Jn. 5:28-29)

Deepen in all of us, Father, a spirit of daring for Your sake.

Old Grocer Fools Burglar

An elderly grocer in Buffalo frightened away a potential burglar with his homemade alarm.

When the gunman threatened to kill him, the self-possessed store owner slid his hand along the counter and pushed a hidden button next to his cash register. This touched off a mechanism he had set up in his front window that sounded exactly like a police-car siren.

That was all the bandit needed. He dropped his gun and made a fast getaway.

Rather than take the defeatist attitude that nothing can be done by the average individual to cope with mounting problems, show a little of the same initiative displayed by the resourceful old grocer.

Don't wait for someone to come along and spell out what you personally can do to right what's wrong with the world. God has entrusted you with imagination. Start putting it to use and you may be happily surprised how many bright ideas you have locked up within you.

What I tell you in the dark, utter in the light; and what you hear whispered, proclaim upon the housetops. (Mt. 10:27)

Stir up within us, Holy Spirit, an ardent desire to be alert on behalf of truth and justice.

Tall Tale Really Wasn't

"Playing with an elephant" was how an 11-year-old youngster in Pasadena, Cal., claimed he had spent his three days as a runaway.

Police investigating the case were skeptical. They thought it was just another tall story from a boy who disappeared after his teacher sent home a poor report card. But they checked anyway.

To their surprise they found an elephant in the exact place specified by the lad. The seven-foot animal was stabled on the outskirts of Pasadena. The owner rented it for movies, parades, and other special events.

Keep children in touch with the countless wonders of nature that God has provided in abundance for the benefit of all of us. By doing so you will contribute much to the development and happiness of youth.

To do otherwise is to deprive them of an important factor in helping them to lead well-balanced and constructive lives.

Unless you turn and become like children, you will never enter the kingdom of heaven. (Mt. 18:3)

Father, give parents the guidance they need to appreciate and foster their children's sense of wonder and play.

Live Up to Your Better Self

This old Swedish proverb deserves at least passing reflection:

Fear less, hope more;
Eat less, chew more;
Whine less, breathe more;
Talk less, love more;
Hate less, love more;
And all good things are yours.

Although there is a bit of Adam and Eve in everyone there is also a divine urge to rise above our weaker tendencies.

By the very nature God gave us we are continually drawn towards living sanely, confidently and constructively. The more each person distinguishes his or her life by faith, hope and charity, the better each functions as well-rounded human beings.

Cultivate in yourself those traits which give outer evidence of your inner nobility and you will appreciate with St. Paul that "all things are yours" both for time and eternity.

All things are yours . . . and you are Christ's; and Christ is God's. (1 Cor. 3:21,23)

Help me to discover in myself, O Lord, Your power to lead a life that honors You and so honors myself and others.

The Hopeful Side of Things

"You know, I think we give too much space in the press to the doings of freaks and crackpots and not enough to those of normal, decent people," a New York newspaper editor told a friend one day in his club.

"Why," he continued, "in New York right now there must be hundreds of thousands of really good people . . . and what's more I'll bet a lot of them are saints and don't know it!"

This incident calls to mind the answer someone once gave when asked the question: "What makes the saints, saints?" The reply given was revealing in its keen insight into human nature, rooted as it is in the divine. It went like this:

"Because they were cheerful, when it was difficult to be cheerful; patient, when it was difficult to be patient; they pushed on, when they wanted to stand still; kept silence, when they wanted to talk; were agreeable, when they wanted to be disagreeable, that was all —

"It was quite simple. And always will be."

Once the millions of good people over the world — everyday "saints" — extend their goodness and become as energetic as the disciples of evil are in reaching out for all humanity, then this tired old earth of ours will be well on the high road to lasting peace.

Great peace have those who love Your law; nothing can make them stumble. (Ps. 119:165)

Give us the grace, Christ Jesus, to bring Your love and truth to everyone rather than keeping it selfishly to ourselves.

What Motive?

In La Rochefoucauld's "Maxims," there is one thought which is particularly worthy of reflection. It goes:

"However brilliant an action, it should not be esteemed great unless the result of a great motive."

Often we hear people say of someone: "He does so much." Yet this may not always be a compliment. While it is certain that idleness is a vice, it is not necessarily true that action is a virtue. The evil-doers of the world are frequently all too active.

The best course is always to act from a motive we can be proud of. To perform a kindness out of love — Christlike love — is the highest behavior.

Just as God so loved the world that He gave His only begotten son to us to purchase our salvation, so should we be inspired in all our actions by love of Him.

That is the Christopher purpose. That is the Christopher motive!

> **When he . . . saw the grace of God, he was glad; and he exhorted them all to remain faithful to the Lord with steadfast purpose. (Acts 11:23)**

Lord, may I always do all things for love of You.

Newspaper Stops Holdup

A bulky Sunday newspaper once stopped a would-be thief in Phoenix.

When the prowler, knife in hand, approached a passer-by and demanded money from him, he got the surprise of his life. The man took his rolled-up newspaper and walloped the thief over the head. The culprit immediately hot-footed it in the other direction.

This was certainly an odd use for a newspaper. The big and important function of the daily press is to bring factual information to countless millions.

Every reader can play a part in furthering the divine standards of truth, charity, and justice which should distinguish a free press.

Help newspapers to grow in dignity and strength so that they may more effectively fulfill their responsibility to the public.

Think of the press as your own, and you will be more apt to protect and further the important service which it can render.

Know the truth and the truth will make you free. (Jn. 8:32)

O Lord, endow all newspaper workers with a deep sense of their responsibility to the public and to the truth.

Helpful Hints for Speakers

Among the do's and don't's that experts recommend to inexperienced public speakers, the following deserve special consideration:

■ Do have something to say before you speak.

■ Don't apologize for your speech. If an excuse is necessary the talk shouldn't be given.

■ Do learn the art of brevity.

■ Don't tell your audience that you won't make a long speech and then proceed to do just that.

■ Don't repeat too much. Say what you have to say — make your point and then move on.

■ Do stop within the time limit given you.

■ Don't encroach upon the time of other speakers. Put yourself in their position.

■ Do adapt yourself to your audience rather than expect them to accommodate themselves to you.

God entrusts you with the power of speech. Whether you use it at home or at an outside meeting, give your listeners something worthwhile and at the same time show respect for their rights and feelings.

Death and life are in the power of the tongue. (Pr. 18:21)

Thanks to You, blessed Creator, for the privileges of being Your instrument in both word and deed.

Postman 'Bites' Dog

A mail carrier in Idaho Falls, Idaho, found that the best way to avoid being nipped by unfriendly dogs is to speak kindly to them. Other postmen might find this attitude a bit too lenient.

For instance, one mailman on Long Island had been bitten by 18 dogs in 17 years. He once received an out-of-court settlement for being bitten four times by a French poodle.

This man now protects himself with an electric dog-training cane. The vibrations at its tip cause antagonistic dogs to remain at a respectful distance.

In dealing with the hostility of man or beast, a combination of firmness and kindness produces the most satisfactory results.

Follow the divine formula of our Savior in meeting the many and varied problems presented by your adversaries. Stand up for principles without compromise but do so in a gentle, loving manner.

Love your enemies and pray for those who persecute you. (Mt. 5:44)

Teach me, Jesus, to disagree without becoming disagreeable.

A Formula for Teaching

Eighty-one-year-old Annie Dakim of Vermont celebrated her 48th year as a teacher by giving her formula for success in the classroom. It is the ability to discover and develop the bit of greatness that God has put in young people.

"Blessed are they who thirst after knowledge of how to direct rather than suppress spontaneous activities of children," Miss Dakim commented.

Teachers find a great challenge in, and enthusiasm for, their work when they realize that every youngster is created in the divine image and has been endowed with a distinct individuality and personality entrusted to no one else.

Encourage a respect and support for all teachers so that they can fulfill the important responsibilities of their noble profession.

> **Those who are wise shall shine like the brightness of the firmament; and those who turn many to righteousness, like the stars forever. (Dan. 12:3)**

> *Grant to all teachers, Divine Teacher, an abundance of consolation in the midst of their strenuous work.*

One Ticket After Another

A motorist in Kansas City had his fill of traffic tickets.

While he was at city hall paying a traffic fine his car was tagged for illegal parking.

When the harassed driver discovered his plight, he took the new ticket down the block to police headquarters.

While explaining his predicament, another patrolman came along and had his car towed away.

Often one little mistake can lead to a multitude of annoying troubles over which one has little or no control.

Over and over again Holy Scripture reminds us to resist the beginnings of wrongdoing, especially in regard to pride, greed, and lust.

More frequently than not a bit of carelessness in this direction opens the way to endless entanglements.

Strive to live up to God's law in even the smallest details and you need have no fear of little problems becoming big ones.

You have been faithful over a little, I will set you over much. (Mt. 25:21)

Help us, Jesus, to be loyal to You in small things as well as large.

Spiritualize Your Organization

Participation in any good organization offers you many opportunities to play the important role of God's instrument in applying His divine truth, justice, and order to human affairs.

▨ Work for high standards despite apathy, misunderstanding, or ingratitude. Such determination can do much to sanctify you as well as your group.

▨ Take the unpopular, thankless jobs — the ones most people avoid, but which must be filled by those with competence and ideals if worthwhile objectives are to be achieved. Remember Christ said: "If any man will come after Me, let him deny himself and take up his cross daily, and follow Me." (Lk. 9:23)

▨ Promote the harmony so necessary for the proper conduct of an organization. Jealousy, wrangling, and bickering weaken that strength which comes only from unity.

How good and pleasant it is when brothers dwell in unity! (Ps. 133:1)

Help us to use every legitimate means, Lord, to sanctify public as well as private life.

The Sound Approach

In 1639 the citizens of Connecticut drew up what has been called "the first written constitution which established a government of free men by themselves."

Like the other founders of our nation, they based government upon God. The document in its original form reads, in part:

"Forasmuch as it hath pleased Almighty God . . . that we . . . are . . . dwelling in and uppon the River of Conectecotte and the Lands thereunto adioyneing; And well knowing where a people are gathered togather the word of God requires that to mayntayne the peace and union of such a people there should be an orderly and decent Government established according to God . . . doe therefore assotiate . . . as one Publike State or Commonwealth; . . ."

Fired with this same spirit, thousands are needed today to participate in the affairs of government. And the urgency now is greater than it was back in the early days of our country. It is up to us!

Give ear, you that rule the people . . . For power is given to you by the Lord. (Wis. 6:34)

Let us pray that those in government will work to preserve our nation "established according to God."

'Greater Love Than This . . .'

A Brooklyn mother was burned to death while saving the lives of her two sons.

When a raging fire broke out in her home, the 36-year-old woman found herself trapped with her two boys, 14 and 12, in a second-story bedroom.

In a desperate attempt to shield her sons from the flames, she flung her body over them.

When firemen arrived, they said they found "flames and smoke so intense we couldn't see six inches in front of our faces. Everything was burning . . . beds, curtains, and furniture."

Groping their way, they stumbled against the body of the mother, slumped over her two sons. The firemen were just in time to save the youngsters but too late for the valiant mother. She had given her life for her children.

The real test of love is not measured in words, but in how much we will sacrifice ourselves in serving God and our fellow human beings.

Let love be genuine. (Rom. 12:9)

Deepen in us, Jesus, such a love for You and everyone that we will sacrifice life itself to prove our love.

Napoleon's Regret

Napoleon made this revealing comment from his exile on the Island of St. Helena:

"Throughout my reign I looked in vain for the man who could rise above routine and think creatively."

Though most people don't realize it, they have the makings of greatness within them. God Himself has given a special ability or talent to every human being. But He leaves it to each one to develop and apply this hidden power in a manner of his or her own choosing.

Human nature is weak, however, and invariably seeks the easy way out. Most of us tend to stay in our comfortable ruts and avoid showing the initiative and imagination of which we are capable.

Once you become convinced that you have an important mission in life to perform for the good of all, you will gladly and even enthusiastically "rise above routine!"

Apathy and inertia will disappear only when you feel that inner compulsion to share with the world the creative power entrusted to you by your Maker.

The sons of this world are more shrewd in dealing with their own generation than the sons of light. (Lk. 16:8)

Deepen in all of us, Creator, a greater desire to put to use the gifts which You have loaned to us.

Are You a Gentle-Man?

It is almost a definition of a gentleman to say he is "one who never inflicts pain," said John Henry Newman, over a hundred years ago.

The true significance of the word "gentleman" is just what it says: a "man" who is "gentle."

Another definition by an unknown author, underlines this fact: "A gentleman is a man who can disagree without being disagreeable."

Few realize the far-reaching good that they can do at home, office, work, in the classroom, on a bus or in a supermarket just by being gentle.

Every one of us can be gentle. We can be instruments of Christ's love by being thoughtful rather than inconsiderate, kindly instead of brusque, patient when it would be so easy to be irritable.

Strive to be a distributor of the divine gentleness that all seek (but too few give) and you will find yourself reaching out to wider horizons as one of God's true gentle-men.

He who does not love his brother whom he has seen, cannot love God whom he has not seen. (1 Jn. 4:20)

Help us, Father, to be instruments of Your love.

How to Stop Rumors

"Even when it brings some truth with it, rumor is not free from the flaw of falsehood, for it ever takes away from, adds to, and alters the truth."

This stern warning was given by Tertullian to the early Christians, and it is one from which all of us can profit.

The following simple rules may help you to be a bearer of "the truth, the whole truth, and nothing but the truth."

■ Think and talk about others with the same sense of accuracy and honesty that you expect of them. Remember Christ's divine standard, so safe and sane:

"As you would that men should do to you, do you also to them in like manner." (Lk. 6:31)

■ Get the facts before allowing yourself to make damaging conclusions based on nothing but half-truths.

■ Focus attention on the good in both individuals and organizations and you will have little time or inclination to be a rumor-monger.

On the day of judgment men will render account for every careless word they utter. (Mt. 12:36)

Let me be so busy speaking about the good in others, Lord, that I may never be a disseminator of unfounded rumors.

Non-Swimming Mother Rescues Child

An expectant mother who couldn't swim saved her 18-month-old son from drowning in Fenton, Mo.

When the young mother's back was turned for a moment, the toddler tumbled off the dock and the current started to carry him down the river.

Although she couldn't swim, she jumped into the water and struck out after her son. She not only reached him 25 feet out in the stream, but even succeeded in getting the nearly drowned tot back to shore.

When her astonished husband was notified at work of his wife's rescue, he exclaimed: "She can't swim!"

Most individuals would be happily surprised at the untouched power for good which God has entrusted to each and every one of them.

Don't wait for an extreme necessity to bring your hidden talent into play. Search for it yourself and begin today to apply it in every way you can. You will be cooperating with the divine plan.

Be strong and of good courage; be not frightened, neither be dismayed for the Lord your God is with you wherever you go. (Jos. 1:9)

Grant me the grace, Holy Spirit, to discover and put to good use the talents which You have loaned to me.

Excuses Seldom Excuse

A new excuse for speeding was submitted by an Ohio motorist who said to the patrolman: "Well, you see officer, the car had been acting up and I wanted to get it home as soon as I could."

The temptation to seek refuge in the assumption that a poor excuse is better than none at all seems like an easy out. But sooner or later, the sobering significance of the old French proverb: "Who excuses, accuses," hits home.

By doing things right in the first place, one can save himself many a lame attempt to gloss over faults or shortcomings.

Even more important, a person who conscientiously lives up to the responsibilities that accompany God-given rights as a homemaker, educator, laborer, merchant or autoist is functioning as a complete human being, as the Creator intended.

In short, live so constructively that you'll not have to think up excuses for yourself or anybody else.

Let us then pursue what makes for peace and for mutual upbuilding. (Rom. 14:19)

Keep me so busy, Lord, doing what is right that I'll not even consider doing otherwise.

How to Keep Fit

The best way to keep a piano in good condition is simply to play it, according to piano manufacturers.

The non-use of a piano impairs it in many ways. Tonal quality suffers. The keys turn yellow and the felted hammers become a target for hungry moths.

With human beings the story is much the same. Failure to use and develop the abilities that God entrusts to each individual usually results in a slow but sure deterioration of the human person.

It is the divine will, then, that we should live fully, not merely exist. Many people go through a whole lifetime without touching or putting to use the bit of greatness within them.

The more we exercise our spiritual, mental, and physical faculties in daily living, the closer we will be to fulfilling the very reason for our existence.

Keep spiritually fit by bringing into daily play the power for good that God expects you to exert.

I came that they may have life, and have it abundantly. (Jn. 10:10)

Let us show appreciation for the gifts of life, Lord, by using, not abusing them.

Purpose Makes the Difference

"Life gets so daily" was the unique expression one housewife used to describe the monotony of her never-ending chores.

Daily routine without high purpose can be not only depressing but actually dangerous.

Boredom is often the breeding ground of endless trouble. It does more than stagnate and poison one person. Its jaundiced outlook can blight the lives of many others as well.

Whether it is your lot in life to drive a bus, wash dishes, write for a newspaper, or work in an office, look at it as a necessary and important step in the business of living, as part of God's plan.

Even the most menial tasks take on new meaning and purpose. Wherever you are, you can reflect the love and glory of God. You can do something to bring joy into the lives of as many as you can reach.

Without that big and stimulating goal, whatever you do will seem a little dull and futile. And life may become very "daily" for you, too.

Trust in the Lord with all your heart, and do not rely on your own insight. In all your ways acknowledge Him and He will make straight your paths. (Pr. 3:5-6)

Grant that I may find the true joy of living, Father, by seeking Your will in all things.

Slow Down and Enjoy Life

Two sailors pedaled their way home from California to North Dakota.

After being discharged from the service in San Francisco, they decided to get a good look at the country on the way home. So they chose to make the trip by bicycle rather than bus, train, or plane.

It took them a month to make the journey. They included a side trip to Vancouver, British Columbia, in order to see relatives.

Few have the time, stamina, or patience to cover 2,000 miles on a bicycle. But nevertheless there is a considerable value in slowing down our pace in one way or another during these hurried times.

Speed for the sake of speed can deprive us of much of the real joy and value of living.

Most of us who are caught up in the rush and distractions of modern times would do well to slow down and enjoy life in the manner God meant us to.

It would also give us more time and a greater inclination to share our blessings with others less fortunate.

A man of quick temper acts foolishly, but a man of discretion is patient. (Pr. 14:17)

Protect me, O Lord, from anything and everything which might separate me from You for eternity.

Every Move Is Watched

Television is playing an unusual role in many jails across the country.

TV cameras, placed at strategic spots throughout the buildings, provide a means of checkup that never existed before.

Every jail cell is within view. Guards can immediately see if anything is amiss. Operations become safer and more efficient, and fewer men are needed to staff a prison.

"The fact that prisoners know they are being watched is more valuable than anything," commented one sheriff.

A vigilant eye, TV or otherwise, is needed to restrain individuals who defy the law. But those who dedicate their lives to good need have no fear of being watched. They have nothing to conceal.

On the contrary, they rejoice in the fact of always living in God's presence and in the realization that a loving Father sees and hears their every thought, prayer, word, and deed.

Nothing is covered up that will not be revealed, or hidden that will not be known. (Lk. 12:2)

Thanks to You, Lord, for the constant joy of being under Your loving eyes.

Too Long in the Back Yard

A traffic accident in North Carolina showed that over-caution can be as dangerous as no caution at all.

One of the drivers involved admitted that it was her first experience driving on a highway. She had previously operated her automobile only in her own back yard.

When the traffic officer asked how long she had been practicing with her car within the confines of her yard, she replied: "Oh, for two or three years."

Playing it safe is a wise policy if it is not carried to extremes. Being over-timid can produce a restricting fear that may keep one from ever tackling the very problem for which one has been preparing.

God wishes you to do more than "brighten your little corner." Unless those of you who are blessed with good ideas and sound principles venture out of your own "back yard," the vast multitude without the knowledge of God's truth and love will never obtain it.

Think, pray and act in terms of all humanity and you yourself will grow in stature.

He who observes the wind will not sow; and he who regards the clouds will not reap. (Ec. 11:4)

Endow us, Divine Redeemer, with the bigness of heart, mind, and soul to reach out to all women and men.

Honoring Parents Has Many Rewards

Mother always comes first with 83-year-old Thomas Johnson of Miami.

While convalescing in Jackson Memorial Hospital following minor surgery, Johnson asked nurses to let him go home. "I've got some important business," he said.

When nurses tactfully inquired what it was, he replied: "I've got to take care of my 115-year-old mother!"

While instances such as this will be few and far between, countless millions of children have endless opportunities to show their parents the love and devotion that are their due.

And by continuing this practice through life they gain far more than they give. The habit of showing thoughtful consideration for parents all through the years brings out a fineness of character, maturity, and nobility that could be achieved in no other way.

When children "young or old, strive conscientiously and continually to "honor" their parents they bring a great blessing on their lives.

Honor your father and your mother. (Ex. 20:12)

Help young people, Divine Master, to show a loving regard for their parents.

No Time to Lose

"Do not squander time, for that is the stuff life is made of." This bit of wisdom was uttered by Benjamin Franklin some 200 years ago.

The precious value of time can never be exaggerated. An hour, minute, or even a second wasted is gone forever. Time lost can never be regained.

If you regard the time you spend on earth as the stepping-stone to eternity, you will automatically want to be a "go-giver" instead of merely a "go-getter."

You won't forget for one moment that eternity depends on how you play your role on the stage of life.

You will realize that the longest life is too short to fulfill the special mission assigned to you by Almighty God Himself — the mission of being an instrument in bringing His divine love, peace, and order to a world very much in need of it.

With the Hebrew psalmist of old you can joyfully say to God:

A thousand years in Your sight are but as yesterday when it is past, or as a watch in the night. (Ps. 90:4)

Instill in each of us, Divine Savior, such a yearning for heaven that we will use every moment on earth to bring Your love to others.

A King Indeed

Frederick the Great of Prussia was walking along a road on the outskirts of Berlin one day when accidentally he brushed against a very old man. "Who are you?" Frederick asked out of idle curiosity as the two came to a halt.

"I am a king," the old man answered.

"A king?" echoed Frederick. "Over what principality do you reign?"

"Over myself," was the proud reply. "I rule myself because I control myself. I am my own subject to command."

All of us can be kings, in the sense of the old man's words. But how many of us actually are? Instead of being in command, often we let ourselves be ruled over by the tyrants of temper or laziness or passion.

We cannot hope to influence others if we are, as the common expression puts it, "not ourselves." And we can only be ourselves by controlling ourselves.

Every athlete exercises self-control in all things. They do it to receive a perishable wreath, but we an imperishable one. (1 Cor. 9:25)

Lord, help me to rule over my passions, that You may rule over me.

More Than Violence Needed

A man who was angered at high taxes took it out on the post office in Sandusky, Ohio.

He broke 12 windows in the building plus two others on a mail truck. Then, in an attempt to show his displeasure in a more dramatic way, he tried unsuccessfully to burn down the post office building.

After his arrest, he explained his strange behavior by saying that he "hated the government because of high taxes and because I can't get a job."

Many a person who objects to taxes may be tempted to express his dissatisfaction in an extreme way. But few problems are settled by violent methods.

Correcting abuses through fair processes of justice and truth requires considerable time, effort, and patience. But, with rare exceptions, it is the only way to avoid totalitarianism.

Protect your blessings by obeying good laws and improving defective ones.

Far be it from us to desert the law and the ordinances. (1 Mac. 2:21)

Impress on me, Spirit of Wisdom, the importance of using true and peaceful methods to correct abuses.

Make Sure You're Right

Out of the War of 1812 came this popular motto, credited to Davy Crockett: "Make sure you are right; then go ahead."

In doing your part to improve the world in which you live you may find some value in the following considerations:

■ If you make sure that your ideas are based on God's truth, you will find that a driving force will carry you through every discouraging obstacle.

■ On the other hand, if you are not sure whether your ideas or plans in regard to important issues are right or wrong, you will be bogged down by your own indecision.

■ Great harm can be done by those who act on mere opinion or emotion, instead of actual fact.

Take the time and effort to root yourself securely in God's truth. This is not only the best way to "make sure you are right" but it will enable you to go ahead with a power and enthusiasm which can be gained in no other way.

Know that the Lord is God; there is no other besides Him. Out of heaven He let you hear His voice, that He might discipline you. (Dt. 4:35-36)

Grant me the grace, Lord, of never fooling myself when distinguishing the big difference between what is right and wrong.

Credit Where It's Due

During a rehearsal of Beethoven's Ninth Symphony the members of the orchestra were so overwhelmingly moved by the conducting of Arturo Toscanini that they rose as one and applauded him. When the spontaneous cheering had subsided Toscanini turned to his orchestra, tears glistening in his eyes.

"Please . . . please! Don't do this!" he said in a pathetic voice. "You see, gentlemen, it isn't me you should applaud. It's Beethoven!"

Cultivate a profound respect for the achievement of others while still retaining a modest awareness of your own accomplishments.

In bearing Christ to those who do not know Him, we can be modest, show them respect, and still never compromise with the Truth. After all, Christ meant their eternal destiny to be the same as ours!

Wisdom from above is first pure, then peaceable, gentle, open to reason, full of mercy and good fruits, without uncertainty or insincerity. And the harvest of righteousness is sown in peace by those who make peace. (Jas. 3:17-18)

Blessed be God; blessed be His Holy Name; blessed be Jesus Christ, true God and true Man.

The Happy Outlook

An old Arabian fable tells of a prince imprisoned in a castle which had 13 windows. Twelve of these windows overlooked lovely scenes, while the 13th looked down on the black ash heaps of the city.

Ignoring the 12 windows, the prince always looked out through the 13th.

It is so often true that whether a person carries with him an atmosphere of gloom and depression or one of confidence and courage depends on his individual outlook.

Of course it isn't always easy to have a cheerful attitude, yet one of the best ways to develop and maintain a reasonably happy view of life is to help those who are troubled and in despair.

One who, with Christ's help, strives to bring light into darkness, health into the midst of disease — to the poor in body and in spirit — inevitably gains much pleasure. His attitude, instead of being morbid, is unfailingly hopeful.

Incline your ear to the poor, and answer him peaceably and gently. Deliver him who is wronged. (Sir. 4:8)

Jesus, grant that I may develop a cheerful outlook on life by bringing cheer to others.

Four Significant Sentences

Basing their authority on God, our Founding Fathers drew up one of the noblest of all documents. In this brief charter they might have referred only once to the Creator. But to underline fundamental truths, which they feared others might discard, they wove into the Declaration of Independence four significant sentences, two at the beginning and two at the end. Each specifically affirms the dependence of every human being on God:

The first reads: "When in the course of human events, it becomes necessary for one people . . . to assume . . . the separate and equal station to which the laws of nature and of nature's God entitle them . . ." Our forefathers emphasized that the natural law itself depends on God.

The second is equally positive: "We hold these truths to be self-evident that all men . . . are endowed by their Creator with certain unalienable rights."

Toward the end of the document the authors appeal "to the Supreme Judge of the world" for the rectitude of their intentions.

The Declaration closes . . . "with a firm reliance on the protection of Divine Providence, we mutually pledge to each other our lives, our fortunes, and our sacred honour."

O God of my fathers and Lord of mercy, (You) have made all things by Your word, and by Your wisdom have formed man to . . . rule the world in holiness and righteousness. (Wis. of Sol. 9:1-3)

Pray and work that these great truths may be brought more and more to the forefront of American life.

'They Labor in Vain'

In 1787, when difficulties arose at the Constitutional Convention in Philadelphia, Benjamin Franklin addressed George Washington, the chairman, in these words:

"The small progress we have made . . . is, methinks, a melancholy proof of the imperfection of the human understanding . . . I have lived, Sir, a long time, and the longer I live, the more convincing proofs I see of this truth, that GOD governs in the affairs of men.

"And if a sparrow cannot fall to the ground without His notice, is it probable that an empire can rise without His aid?

"We have been assured, Sir, in the Sacred Writings, that 'except the Lord build the House, they labor in vain that built it.' I firmly believe this; and I also believe that, without His concurring aid, we shall succeed in this political building no better than the builders of Babel."

The sense of dependence on God that motivated the founders of our country should be a characteristic of every true American today — tomorrow — always!

Unless the Lord builds the house, those who build it labor in vain. Unless the Lord watches over the city the watchman stays awake in vain. (Ps. 127:1)

Pray that we may always work to preserve the democracy that God's Providence has given us.

How to Sleep Better

A small hotel at the edge of the Rocky Mountains advertises the privacy and peace of its air-conditioned rooms with this quip: "If you can't sleep here, it's your conscience."

There may be many other reasons why a person will toss and turn at night. But nobody will deny that a good conscience goes a long way toward ensuring a restful night.

Moreover, a right heart keeps one in the right frame of mind all day long.

Many persons are constantly searching for peace of mind and soul, unaware that the answer is within themselves — in a good conscience.

A maxim that the teenaged George Washington inscribed in his notebook merits reflection: "Labor to keep alive in your breast that little spark of celestial fire called conscience."

Live by principle and you will better yourself and become a more effective instrument in applying God's truth to human affairs.

(Love) issues from a pure heart and a good conscience and sincere faith. (1 Tim. 1:5)

Grant me, Holy Spirit, that I may always enjoy a good conscience.

The Lady With the Lamp

The example of Florence Nightingale is a good one. Born to comfort and social position, she gave up everything to serve those who needed her help. The inspiring words of her "Pledge" are worth reflection:

"I solemnly pledge myself before God and in the presence of this assembly:

"To pass my life in purity and to practice my profession faithfully.

"I will abstain from whatever is deleterious and mischievous, and will not take or knowingly administer any harmful drug.

"I will do all in my power to elevate the standard of my profession, and will hold in confidence all personal matters committed to my keeping and all family affairs coming to my knowledge in the practice of my profession.

"With loyalty will I endeavor to aid the physician in his work, and devote myself to the welfare of those committed to my care."

Come, O blessed of My Father, inherit the kingdom prepared for you from the foundation of the world; for . . . I was sick and you visited Me. (Mt. 25:34,36)

Divine Physician, give every nurse an appreciation of her sacred profession.

You Are at Least One

If you are tempted to feel sorry for yourself, or let that futile sense of "I don't count" creep over you, take a minute to reflect on this wise old saying:

"I am only one, but I am one. I cannot do everything, but I can do something. What I can do, I ought to do. And what I ought to do, by the grace of God I will do."

In short, don't underestimate your importance in the divine plan. Even though you may seldom give it a thought, it is both inspiring and sobering to realize that the Lord actually sends some of His blessings to others through you. Don't deprive them of what is rightfully theirs.

What you do — or fail to do — by prayer, word, and deed to see that God's will is done "on earth as it is in heaven" affects the well-being of everyone to some degree.

Yes, the world itself can be a little better or a little worse because you have been in it. It's up to you to decide which it will be.

Who does the will of God abides for ever. (1 Jn. 2:17)

Thanks to You, Divine Master, for allowing me to play a small role in bringing peace to everyone.

His Peanuts Were Hot

Business is business with a 12-year-old boy in Montgomery, Ala.

The youngster had built up quite a little enterprise in the summer selling peanuts.

But soon competition came from his younger brother. He set himself up in the peanut business, too, and lost no time in approaching any and every prospect within reach.

The older brother took to the telephone to keep his regular customers. His selling argument to the news editor of the local newspaper was brief and to the point: "My peanuts are hot. My brother's are cold. Wait for mine!"

Healthy competition can do much to stimulate imagination, enterprise, and initiative. But make sure that any efforts to further your own interests are based on the sound principles of charity and justice.

You will bring God's blessing on your efforts if you seek the good of others as well as your own.

Do no wrong in judgment, in measures of length or weight or quantity . . . have just balances, just weights. (Lev. 19:35-36)

Let me be guided by a sense of Your own fairness, Lord, in all that I do.

Develop Your Speaking Ability

A copy book found in a Pharaoh's tomb contained this bit of advice, written 3,000 years ago:

"Make yourself a craftsman in speech for thereby you shall gain the upper hand. The tongue of man is his weapon and speech is mightier than fighting."

Most people never realize the tremendous power entrusted to them by God through the faculty of speech. And yet 90 percent of their communication with others is through the spoken word.

Check up on yourself. Note how many opportunities you have each day to improve your speaking ability: when you talk to your family; make a telephone call; swap ideas at school; explain work procedures in your shop or farm; or discuss the merits of an issue or candidate for public office.

If you strive to make yourself a craftsman in speech you will exert a far greater influence for peace in a world much in need of every assistance that one person like you can provide.

Wisdom, is known through speech, and education through the words of the tongue. (Sir. 4:24)

Creator, thank You for the power of speech: help me always to put it to good use.

Still Serving at 91

A 91-year-old woman in Phoenix was excused from jury duty when the judge discovered her age.

But she didn't agree with his reasoning: "Who wants to be excused? I want to serve," she insisted.

Those who gladly and generously serve the common good actually rejuvenate themselves as well. They live more meaningful and often longer lives.

On the other hand, those who cautiously dodge duties and responsibilities that benefit others actually cheat themselves out of the fullness of living that God wishes all of us to enjoy.

Seek practical outlets for that particular service which you and you alone can render to the common good of all.

If you truly "want to serve," as this 91-year-old woman did, you will not let personal inconvenience discourage or stop you.

You will regard it as a small price to pay for the joy that will be yours both here and hereafter.

Through love be servants of one another. For the whole law is fulfilled in one word, "You shall love your neighbor as yourself." (Gal. 5:13-14)

May I be ever aware, Lord, that by serving others I serve You, too.

Unkind Speech Led Him to Despair

Clinging precariously to the girders of the Williamsburg Bridge in Manhattan, a 34-year-old man threatened to jump and wash away what he called a rotten life.

Two policeman spotted him and began to inch their way toward him on his dizzying perch some 200 feet above the busy roadway.

As they drew closer, one of them engaged him in small talk, causing him to hesitate until they were close enough to prevent him from jumping.

On the way to the hospital for observation, the would-be suicide said he tried to kill himself because: "I hurt too many people by saying the wrong things."

The power of words, for good or evil, cannot be exaggerated. A loving Creator has given us the power of speech to praise Him and to share the truth with all.

Use it well and you will never experience the remorse of those who say the wrong things when they should say the right things.

If any one thinks he is religious, and does not bridle his tongue . . . this man's religion is vain. (Jas. 1:26)

Help me to speak always with humility, sincerity and a desire to support and encourage others, Jesus.

One Big Pull

Six-year-old Johnny proved he could read recently. Anxious to demonstrate how well he had learned his first-grade lesson, he saw a handle marked in big letters "pull." He did what it said.

Results were more than he bargained for. Three thousand students marched out of their classrooms for the first fire drill of the semester.

Youngsters have a unique way of giving outward expression to their inner power. This irrepressible energy may be applied in strange ways, to be sure. But we shouldn't forget that it can likewise be channeled in the right direction almost as easily as it finds an outlet in mischievous ways.

Humankind is much in need of the hope, zest, and enthusiasm with which God has blessed youth in such abundance.

Nurture rather than repress this power in each child and it may do much to renew the face of the earth.

Let the children come to Me, do not hinder them; for to such belongs the kingdom of God. (Mk. 10:14)

Help us all to discover and develop the greatness in every young person, Jesus.

Once We Wake Up

At the end of World War I there was a loud cry that Christianity had failed. Promptly G. K. Chesterton, the great English writer, took those who held this view to task.

"The trouble with Christianity is, not that it's failed," he said, "but that it's never been tried . . . not that it can't remake the world, but that it's difficult."

If everyone who has the privilege of Christian training and the grace to adhere to it were to make use of Christ's principles in every walk of life, we should soon see Christianity changing the face of the globe.

The devil, knowing this, keeps alive the fiction that it is impossible to bring high ideals into the workaday world, and the enemies of Christ make it their business always to proclaim that Christianity won't work.

Yet, despite this, the one thing that terrifies the godless the world over is the fear that some day those who believe in Christ will wake up — and start acting their beliefs. Once that happens, most of the great problems which plague humanity will disappear overnight.

We have our hope set on the living God, who is the Savior of all. (1 Tim. 4:10)

May strength and courage be ours, Father, to work as if the salvation of the world depended totally on us.

Stops Driving at 81

An 81-year-old woman surprised officials by turning in her driver's license in Albany.

The octogenarian had a perfect driving record. But she returned her license to the State Motor Vehicle Bureau with this thoughtful comment:

"It would be a nice gesture to turn in my license and retire from driving a car voluntarily before I might become a menace to life on the highway."

To have the wisdom and courage to acknowledge one's limitations is a tribute to anyone, old or young. It is even more commendable when such self-restraint shows a consideration for the well-being of others.

God has put it within the power of every one of us to contribute to the well-being of humanity by doing good and avoiding evil.

The more we realize that the peace of the world starts with each of us, the more alert we will probably be in thinking up practical ways to apply divine law and order to human affairs.

Thy will be done on earth as it is in heaven. (Mt. 6:10)

Deepen in me, Father, a greater thoughtfulness of others.

A Vicious Cycle

There is an old saying that goes:

> *"Peace begets prosperity;*
> *Prosperity begets pride;*
> *Pride begets prejudice;*
> *Prejudice begets war;*
> *War begets poverty."*

The thoughts expressed here may be an over-simplification of specific problems. Yet one transition — that of prosperity to pride — seems especially insidious.

Prosperity should offer us opportunities to extend our interest in others. Yet, paradoxically, prosperity often begets self-interest — a desire to advance our own welfare, oblivious of our relationship to others.

Christ's balance wheel is safe and sane: "Love thy neighbor as thyself." We are expected to take care of ourselves, of course. But that doesn't mean we should spend 98 percent of our thought and time on ourselves, especially when He favors us with prosperity. When we do, the trouble begins: "Pride begets prejudice; prejudice begets war; war begets poverty."

Love is patient and kind; love is not jealous or boastful; it is not arrogant or rude. Love does not insist on its own way; it is not irritable or resentful. (1 Cor. 13:4-5)

Help us, Lord, in our proud prosperity to remember the adversities of others.

Long-Lost Money Returns

It took 10 years for a missing $10 bill to find its way back to its rightful owner, a woman in Uniontown, Pa.

An unsigned note accompanied the lost and long-forgotten money. It read:

"Quite a few years ago I found your wallet. I should have returned it to you then. But I had four small children and it was near Christmas, so I used the money. I hope you will forgive me."

An example like this is heartwarming evidence that human beings, despite their shortcomings, retain, through thick and thin, some bit of God-given goodness.

It usually takes a long time and much effort for those who have made mistakes to rise above their weaknesses. But it is most reassuring to know that in even the worst there is an inclination to right what is wrong.

Countless opportunities are open to every one of us to nurture and develop this divine spark in every human being. In every attempt to uncover it we are imitating the Redeemer Himself.

The righteous live for ever and their reward is with the Lord; the Most High takes care of them. (Wis. of Sol. 5:15)

Bless, Holy Spirit, those who, despite obstacles, prove their honesty.

One Snake Too Many

Having a five-foot boa constrictor slither across the kitchen floor was the last straw for one housewife in Washington, D.C.

She knew that her 12-year-old son had been "boarding" a small assortment of pets for a 16-year-old neighbor. But she hadn't paid much attention until the boa constrictor appeared on the scene. She wasted no time in investigating further.

To her amazement she found her home was harboring a small menagerie: one rabbit, five turtles, nine lizards, two more snakes, and one birdcage.

A few more inquiries disclosed that the boy next door had stolen them from the pet shop where he worked. He gave as his reason "love of animals."

Liking animals is commendable. But it is no excuse for stealing them. The end, no matter how worthy, never justifies using questionable means to attain it.

In all that you think, say, and do, strive to be truthful and you will honor God and automatically respect the rights of others.

Every one who is of the truth hears My voice. (Jn. 18:37)

Let me ever remember that I am always in Your presence, Jesus.

Littering Brings Punishment

Seven teenagers in New Jersey learned a lesson the hard way.

While riding along in a bus they tore up magazines and tossed the pieces out the window.

A city official, who happened to see them littering the streets, stopped the bus and gave the boys an assignment they will not forget in a hurry.

He ordered them to pick up every piece of paper, cigarette butt, and matchstick over a three-block area. He himself remained to make sure they completed the job.

Whether littering a street or committing a petty misdemeanor, the average offender is seldom malicious in the beginning. A penalty in time can often nip dangerous tendencies in the bud and save someone from slipping into bad habits, even a life of crime.

It is better still to help those responsible for trouble to channel their destructive tendencies into worthwhile channels.

God will bless you if you strive to find the element of good in every person and build on that.

Depart from evil, and do good; seek peace, and pursue it. (Ps. 34:15)

Grant me the grace, loving Savior, to confess my faults, do penance, and amend my life.

The Problem Remains

When the Duke of Windsor was Prince of Wales he once visited, in the same afternoon, the newly built steamship Queen Mary and some Glasgow slums.

Afterward he said to a friend: "How do you reconcile a world that has produced that mighty ship with the slums we have just visited?"

A British scientist, after hearing this remark, observed: "That is the problem that we have to solve, and it is useless to go out and solve scientific problems if you cannot solve that."

In our pride in technological advances we must not forget that there are many who are in misery the world over. The invention of a new kind of washing machine, for example, means little to the person who has no clothes.

If we are enjoying a life of comforts, we should be particularly solicitous about others, making sure that we are not forgetting our responsibilities toward our neighbors.

You shall love your neighbor as yourself. Love does no wrong to a neighbor; therefore love is the fulfilling of the law. (Rom. 13:9-10)

Creator, teach me to help those who suffer privation.

On Pride

A device the Devil uses with great success when he wishes to cripple a worthy project is the stirring up of petty pride among those concerned. This is an evil which, by infecting even one or two, can nip in the bud the most promising enterprise for good.

And, with typical deception, this type of deadly pride, which aims at tripping up high-minded persons and ruining much good that could be done, persists in the name of virtue. As the poet Coleridge well said:

> *And the Devil did grin, for his darling sin*
> *Is pride that apes humility.*

Since this treacherous vice so often appears in harmless garb and manifests itself in so many disguises, we should be especially alert to see that we do not succumb to it ourselves.

We can better avoid the pitfalls of pride by concentrating our minds and hearts on the practice of true humility which is rooted in the knowledge that all we are and all we have comes from God.

He who abides in Me, and I in him . . . bears much fruit, for apart from Me you can do nothing. (Jn. 15:5)

Jesus, may I be ever conscious that without Your aid I can achieve nothing.

The Courage to Say No

Many observers fear that the self-indulgence and moral indifference spreading over the world may destroy freedom. Walter Lippmann put it this way:

"Without order or authority in the spirit of man the free way of life leads through weakness, disorganization, self-indulgence, and moral indifference to the destruction of freedom itself.

"The tragic ordeal through which the Western world is passing was prepared in the long period of easy liberty, during which men . . . forgot that their freedom was achieved by heroic sacrifice . . . They forgot that their rights were founded on their duties . . . they thought it clever to be cynical and enlightened to be unbelieving, and sensible to be soft."

Most of us know we must bring forth fruit worthy of penance; that with God's help we must be firm when tempted to be weak; that we must have the courage to say "No" when it would be easy to say "Yes." Knowing this, we ought — if we wish to preserve our sacred freedom — to help bring order and discipline into the main stream of life.

Bear fruit that befits repentance. (Mt. 3:8)

Author of our liberties, help us use the talents You have given us to preserve our precious heritage of freedom.

Much of the World in the Dark

Almost 70 percent of the world's people live their lives without knowing what's going on at home or abroad, according to a survey.

In the countries of Africa, Asia and Latin America, fewer than 10 copies of daily newspapers are available for each 100 persons. Not quite five in every 100 have radio receivers and less than two have television sets.

Experts look upon this lack of information as a deterrent to education and to technical and professional instruction as well.

Well-informed public opinion is essential to the growth of freedom in newly developing nations. Encourage competent and rightly motivated persons to help people the world over to exercise their God-given right to know about the world we live in.

Do what you can to encourage young people to enter careers that will promote the intellectual and eternal good of all. In doing so you will imitate Him who is the "Light of the world."

If you continue in My word . . . you will know the truth, and the truth will make you free. (Jn. 8:31)

Enable me to make knowledge serve Your truth and not oppose it, Jesus.

Talents Being Wasted

Between 20 and 30 percent of the nation's most talented students are wasting their abilities by not using them fully.

The "underachiever," one who habitually fails to perform anywhere near his or her scholastic ability, frequently gets off to a bad start in the earliest grades.

Experts have observed that improper attitudes toward school work have a tendency to mar a person's entire future life.

The cooperation of parents, teachers, school authorities and the motivation of the students themselves all go into excellence in education.

Even if you are not directly involved in this vital field, it is still your concern. Do your best for God and country by encouraging the goal of excellence in teachers and students. And work for adequate educational facilities.

It is a crime to waste the minds of our most talented students.

(Make) your ear attentive to wisdom and (incline) your heart to understanding. (Prov. 2:2)

Enable me, Divine Teacher, to respect intellectual and spiritual values and to show others how to have those same values.

Good Water, a Priceless Asset

When you take a drink of water do you ever reflect on what a blessing it really is? Here are some facts on this precious substance:

■ Impure water was the main cause of a cholera epidemic which sickened at least 42,000 people in Asia.

■ More children die of diarrhea over the world than any other malady. Experts say that between 30 and 60 percent of such deaths could be prevented by pure drinking water.

■ The danger of typhoid, trachoma and yaws would also be greatly reduced by pure water.

■ Nearly 40 percent of the people in Latin American towns are without adequate water supplies.

You can do much to relieve the world-wide shortage of this priceless and lifegiving liquid. Conserve water and do not contribute to its pollution. Encourage government, industry, science and education to tackle the vital concerns of a pure water supply and water conservation.

Even if only one in 10,000 persons dedicated themselves to this Christlike work, both the physical and spiritual troubles of the world would be greatly eased.

The man who trusts in the Lord . . . is like a tree planted by water, that sends out its roots by the stream, and does not fear when heat comes for its leaves remain green, and is not anxious in the year of drought, for it does not cease to bear fruit. (Jer. 17:7-8)

God, help me to appreciate Your gift of water.

There Is Good in Everyone

"There is no surprise more magical than the surprise of being loved," Charles Morgan once said. "It is the finger of God on a man's shoulder."

There's a bit of nobility in the worst of human beings because all are made in God's image and that image can never be completely effaced or lost. Even those who have decided to have nothing whatsoever to do with God aren't frozen in that state of mind. Deep in the roots of their being — just because they are created in the divine image — there is an ever-present tug toward their Maker.

It is the privilege of Christ-bearers to help them become aware of this tremendous attraction. You can honestly say to anyone, with little danger of hurting his or her feelings: "There's a lot of good in you!" With a kind word or a friendly glance you can do much to inspire confidence. Never write anybody off!

No matter how desperate the case, no matter how ignoble the character, let yours be the unshakable conviction that there is always hope!

> You have put off the old nature with its practices and put on the new nature which is being renewed in knowledge after the image of its Creator. Here there cannot be Greek and Jew, circumcised and uncircumcised, barbarian, Scythian, slave, free man, but Christ is all, and in all. (Col. 3:9-11)

> *Lord, help us to see Your image in each human being and to love them because they are made by You and for You.*

Honesty Starts With You

"Make yourself an honest man, and then you may be sure that there is one rascal less in the world." These words of Thomas Carlyle give each of us a ready starting point and a final goal in our life.

Look up "honest" in the dictionary. You will find the word means: "honorable, hence creditable; is characterized by integrity and straightforwardness in thought, speech and implies a refusal to lie, steal, or deceive in any way; denotes free from fraud, genuine, open and frank in relations with others."

How many of these virtues apply to you, and your dealings with others? If you remember that honesty in the world starts with you, you will be less inclined to complain about corruption and graft in public affairs and more likely to take steps to correct such abuses in a constructive way.

Make it a practice to be honest in thought, word and deed and you will please both God and man. Remember that you can't force others, but you can force yourself to be honest.

If you continue in My word, you are truly My disciples, and you will know the truth, and the truth will make you free. (Jn. 8:32)

May I honor You, heavenly Father, by being honest with everyone.

Start Early With Children

One woman was especially attentive while a noted educator was giving a lecture on the importance of training children at an early age.

After the talk, she came up to the podium and asked him, "How early can I begin the education of my child?"

"When will your child be born?" he queried.

"Born?" she gasped. "Why, he is already five years old."

"My goodness, woman," he cried, "don't just stand there talking to me. Hurry home — you have already lost five years."

Difficult as it is for us to realize, a tiny baby in the crib is even then beginning to take on the outlook and character that will shape his or her life and eternity.

The privilege entrusted to parents by the Creator demands that fathers and mothers devote much time and attention to their children. No amount of trinkets or baubles can replace parental love.

> **Do not provoke your children to anger, but bring them up in the discipline and instruction of the Lord. (Eph. 6:4)**

> *Inspire all who are blessed with children, Father, to give them the attention that is their due.*

Juror Fretted About Canaries

Canaries have to eat, too, insisted a juror in Lockport, N.Y.

He complained to officials that the prolonged deliberation of a case had kept him in court for two days and his birds were going hungry.

To solve the problem a patrol car was sent to the man's home. The deputy who fed the canaries reported to the court that he left the birds "chirping happily."

Countless people display a devoted interest in birds. But all of it put together pales in comparison to the astounding "feeding job" that the Lord Himself does in His divine solicitude for billions of birds the world over.

Yet as much as God loves all creatures, He loves you far more. He Himself stresses that you personally are "of much more value than they."

> **Look at the birds of the air: they neither sow nor reap nor gather into barns, and yet your heavenly Father feeds them. Are you not of more value than they? (Mt. 6:26)**

Thanks to You, O Heavenly Father, for Your loving solicitude for all Your Creation.

You Need to Be Needed

"I miss being needed," was the significant complaint made by a 40-year-old wife and mother.

She suddenly realized that her grown family depended on her less and less. She had raised them to think for themselves and stand on their own two feet. And they were doing just that.

They were still thoughtful of her, to be sure, but gradually and quite naturally they stopped turning to her in their needs and problems.

"To realize that you're not really needed is a great blow," the woman commented. "There must be something I can do to fill that void — I still can be of service to others."

None of us is really content unless we give and keep giving of ourselves. God made us that way.

But the Lord does not spell out how, when, and where each of us can make our own particular contribution. He wants us to prove our love for Him and others by discovering the most effective outlet for the goodness within us.

Cast your bread upon the waters. (Ec. 11:1)

Empower me, O Lord, to spend and be spent in a life-long service to others.

The Earthworm's Contribution

Lowly earthworms perform an important service to humankind. They maintain productive soils by mixing organic material near the surface with the vital particles underlying it.

Scientists claim that millions of earthworms in an acre of good ground can bring approximately 20 tons of buried soil to the surface each year.

Quietly but persistently they dig their way through the earth, transporting small portions of it from one level to another and cementing together various soil particles. This produces a well-aerated and well-drained soil for both farmer and forester.

You will find countless testimonies in nature to the fabulous plan of the Creator. Whether it is the insignificant earthworm, an eagle soaring through the air, a whale singing in the depths of the seas, or the sun warming the earth, each reflects the glory and majesty of God.

The heavens are telling the glory of God; and the firmament proclaims His handiwork.

Thanks to You, bountiful Father, for the endless blessings of Your creation.

True Joy Is Something Special

The word joy is mentioned in the Bible more than 130 times. God wants us to lead lives that are truly joyous.

But His concept of joy is quite different from what the world calls pleasure.

Joy is identified with the heart, mind, and soul. It has a deep, lasting, even eternal quality and can carry a person through hardship and suffering. Christ said: "You . . . have sorrow now: but I will see you again, and your heart shall rejoice, and your joy no one shall take from you." (Jn. 16:22)

Pleasure, on the other hand, is usually connected with physical or material things. Helpful and useful as it is, it can be fleeting, illusive, and even joyless, especially when pursued for its own sake. St. Paul went so far as to say: "She who gives herself up to pleasures is dead while she is still alive." (1 Tim. 5:6)

Rejoice in the Lord always; again I will say, Rejoice. . . . The Lord is at hand. Have no anxiety about anything, but in everything by prayer and supplication with thanksgiving let your requests be made known to God. (Phil. 4:4)

Let me be Your instrument, Savior, in bringing joy where there is sadness and anxiety.

Saved by the Rules

Some young sailors avoided a major tragedy during a race on Long Island Sound because they obeyed a basic principle of sailing.

When a sudden and violent squall caught the fleet of 113 small racing boats by surprise, half of them turned over. More than 100 youngsters, aged 9 to 17, were tumbled into the storm-lashed waters.

Turbulent winds and five-foot waves scattered the boats in all directions over a two-mile area.

But there was no loss of life. All the youngsters stayed by their capsized boats. They had been taught over and over again that their craft would float even when filled with water. Every one of the young sailors clung to their overturned boats until they were rescued.

Keep yourself ever conscious of eternal principles and they will buoy you up through every storm of life and bring you a deep sense of peace and security.

Because you are precious in My eyes, and honored, and I love you . . . fear not, for I am with you. (Is. 43:4-5)

May Your divine truth, O Lord, be my strength and shield in fair weather and foul.

Yours for the Asking

How would you like to have a coal mine and a gas well in your own back yard?

A Kentucky farmer can claim that unusual advantage. All his life he has been shoveling whatever coal he needs from a vein near his house. His father did the same before him. Two days of digging provide him with enough coal for an entire winter!

His supply of natural gas comes from a well originally drilled by prospectors who abandoned it when no oil turned up.

Few people are fortunate enough to have their utility needs met so cheaply. But everyone, without exception, can benefit from the endless supply of spiritual power that is within praying distance of each one of us. All we need to do is ask the Lord for it. It is ours for the asking.

Develop a closer relationship with Christ, your Redeemer, through the intimacy of brief prayers, offered frequently throughout each day. You will deepen and increase your spiritual power if you do.

I urge that supplications, prayers, intercessions and thanksgivings be made for all . . . that we may lead a quiet and peaceable life, godly and respectful in every way. (1 Tim. 2:1)

Thank You, Holy Paraclete, for making it so easy for me to draw my power from You.

The Bride Fainted

A young engineer in Spain walked out on his own wedding. When asked if he wished to take the bride for his lawful wife, he answered: "Frankly, no!"

The bride fainted. The groom disappeared out of the church door.

A week later the young man changed his mind. To the delight of his friends, as well as his bride, he replied with a ringing "yes" to the same question.

Long before the wedding day all fundamental doubts should be happily resolved. Marriage is an important step and affects the destiny of so many people "for better or for worse."

It deserves and requires serious, adequate preparation. To rush into it or to take its serious consequences lightly can handicap a marriage from the very start.

Do your part to promote a greater respect for holy matrimony. Remind others that it is an institution of God Himself. He expects us to bring to it both the natural and spiritual qualities that will ensure both joy and permanence.

A man leaves his father and his mother and cleaves to his wife, and they become one flesh. (Gen. 2:24)

Bless those, Jesus, who faithfully live up to their marriage vows.

Don't Let Criticism Stop You

"The dogs bark, but the caravan moves on" is an age-old proverb that has a valuable lesson for those bothered by unfair criticism.

When the big caravan stops even momentarily to argue with the little dogs, it suffers two losses. Progress is held up and the barking is usually increased rather than lessened.

The next time friend or foe heckles you unfairly, pleasantly ignore it and keep merrily "moving on" about your business. Unjust criticism or fault-finding invariably ceases when it is not contested.

Just as dogs eventually stop barking when nobody pays attention to them, so do chronic critics drop their complaining if they are not taken seriously or are disregarded altogether.

Be true to God, to yourself and to others in pursuing your mission in life and no amount of criticism will ever dissuade you, much less stop you.

The devising of folly is sin, and the scoffer is an abomination. (Prov. 24:9)

Teach me, Jesus, to rise above petty criticism.

This Way to Heaven

"What is the one big request of your life?" was the question asked of an elderly nurse on a TV program.

Her answer came as a surprise to many listeners. She said: "To meet my Lord and Savior Jesus Christ and hear Him say that He thinks I did a good job for Him during my stay on earth."

Millions who heard this heartwarming profession of faith had good reason to pause and reflect. Behind her words was a lifetime of self-less service which had often lacked the comforts and pleasures some consider essential for happiness.

And yet her joyful attitude, so evident on the television screen, revealed that her sacrifices had been worthwhile and had brought her a share in that "peace which the world cannot give and which the world cannot take away."

Those who take the long-range view and keep ever conscious of the one big goal of life are blessed with an inner joy and sense of security that finds outward expression in all they say and do.

Fret not yourself over him who prospers in his way, . . . who carries out evil devices! . . . For the wicked shall be cut off; but those who wait for the Lord shall possess the land. (Ps. 37:7,8)

Help me, Divine Lord, to accomplish much good during my stay on earth.

Thieves Haven't Got a Chance

Television is now protecting Cleveland art galleries from thieves. Thirty-three cameras were installed in the Museum of Art to help guards to supervise all eight galleries at one time.

No matter where a thief may be, he is quickly detected and a warning can be relayed over the loud-speaker system. Though a robber might try to escape to another room, he remains ever in view on the TV screen.

It is a never-ending task to promote good and prevent evil. If you see defects in vital areas, let the very misdeeds remind you that your good efforts are needed more than ever.

Remember that by doing nothing positive and constructive you may be helping to further the very abuses of which you disapprove.

He who is not with Me is against Me, and he who does not gather with Me scatters. (Mt. 12:30)

Enable me to be a "doer" of Your will, Lord, rather than a mere fault-finder.

Creative Outlet for Ex-Forger

An ex-forger not only mended his ways while behind prison bars but developed an artistic talent that helped prepare him for a useful life when he left jail.

During his confinement, the 54-year-old man designed, executed and installed stained glass windows in the chapels at Sing Sing and Dannemora.

The judge who signed his release said: "I have examined your work with awe . . . You did a remarkable job of showing Christianity at work."

Rather than allow people who have made mistakes to become even worse, take whatever steps you can to help them rehabilitate themselves.

It is not easy to shift into worthwhile channels talent that has been used for wrong-doing. But every effort you make to redeem one person who has been the victim of his or her own weakness will not only solve many problems but will also release creative talent that God intended to be used to help, not hurt.

Whoever brings back a sinner from the error of his way will save his soul from death and will cover a multitude of sins. (Jas. 5:20)

Let me become so interested in doing good, Jesus, that I will be little inclined to do evil.

Lincoln Gave a Warning

That government "is your business" was the point hammered home by President-elect Abraham Lincoln in a speech at Indianapolis, Feb. 11, 1861. He was en route to Washington to take his oath of office. Here is a portion of that famous talk:

"I wish you to remember, now and forever, that it is your business, and not mine; that if the union of these States and the liberties of these people shall be lost, it is but little to any one man of 52 years of age, but a great deal to the 30 millions of people who inhabit these United States, and to their posterity in all coming time.

"It is your business to rise up and preserve the Union and liberty for yourselves, and not for me.

"I appeal to you again to constantly bear in mind that not with politicians, not with Presidents, not with office-seekers, but with you, is the question: Shall the Union and shall the liberties of this country be preserved to the latest generations?"

God expects you to make government your business.

You were called to freedom, brethren; . . . through love be servants of one another. (Gal. 5:13)

Keep me mindful of the responsibilities that accompany the blessings of freedom, Divine Liberator.

A Modest Hero

No one knew the name of the man who rescued a 10-month-old baby from a burning building in North Hollywood, Cal. In the excitement, he left without identifying himself.

When the modest man got home, he casually told his wife and children about the incident. Next day when newspapers hailed the unknown hero, his 11-year-old son, a newsboy, decided to call the paper with this information.

"I see you want to know the man who saved that baby. Well, he's my Dad!" He then gave the name of his father, Lee Ritchie, 39, a store manager and father of three.

You can be quite sure that your motives are nobly high if you are willing to be considerably inconvenienced in serving others and to be forgotten yourself. God sees what you do and that counts more than any amount of personal recognition.

When you give alms, do not let your left hand know what your right hand is doing, so that your alms may be in secret; and your Father who sees in secret will reward you. (Mt. 6:3-4)

Teach me the wisdom, Holy Spirit, of seeking the good of others even though I am forgetting myself.

Don't Bury Your Talent

If you had $100,000 would you bury it in your back yard? One man did that years ago in Chicago. He hid his treasure — a collection of gold coins — under two fruit trees at the rear of his suburban home.

Executors of his estate found the first clue in a scribbled note on a desk pad. This led to the discovery of a small safe in the garage. A map was found in it showing the exact location of the gold cache.

It took only a little digging to unearth the treasure that had been long out of circulation.

Those who bury any kind of talent — physical, intellectual or spiritual — seldom realize that it prevents it from benefiting anyone.

In the parable of the talents (Mt. 25:14-38) our Lord praised those who put their God-given ability to work. But he condemned the man who buried even one talent.

> **Why then did you not put my money into the bank, and at my coming I should have collected it with interest? (Lk. 19:23)**

Help me, O Lord, to use for the good of others the talents You have loaned me.

Baby Rescued From Garbage

A newborn baby was found one wintry day in a garbage truck seconds before it would have been crushed to death in the truck's compacting mechanism.

This discarded infant had originally been dropped into a refuse can which in turn had been emptied into the garbage truck.

The baby, blue with cold, was rushed to the nearest hospital where it responded to treatment.

A nurse said the tiny boy must have been in excellent condition at birth to survive the cold and harsh treatment he had to endure.

Thank God, a case such as this is a rarity. However, it does indicate a dangerous trend which treats human beings without the respect and honor their nature demands.

Do everything in your power to protect and deepen the reverence for even the least individual. What you do or fail to do to promote the worth of human beings as individuals made in God's image, can make a big difference.

Whoever gives you a cup of water to drink because you bear the name of Christ, will by no means lose his reward. (Mk. 9:41)

Give me the wisdom and strength, Lord God, to champion the rights which You have given to every individual.

Young People Need Inspiration

Thomas Edison sent the following recommendations to a youth assembly that requested a message from him:

■ "Always be interested in whatever you undertake, or may be doing for the moment . . .

■ "Don't mind the clock, but keep at it, and let nature indicate the necessity of rest . . .

■ "Failures, so called, are but finger posts pointing out the right direction to those who are willing to learn.

■ "Hard work and a living general interest in everything that makes for human progress will make men or women more valuable and acceptable to themselves and to the world."

Young people are more likely to devote time and energy more generously to a constructive life if they are motivated by a noble, Christ-like sense of purpose. Let them know they can be co-workers with God in helping humanity and you will truly inspire them.

Who sows bountifully will also reap bountifully. (1 Cor. 9:6)

Enable parents, teachers and all others, Father, to bring out the hidden greatness in youth.

Charge as You Would Be Charged

It was cheaper up than down for 20 persons who wanted to get a good view of the Tournament of Roses parade in Pasadena some years ago.

They paid 50 cents each for the privilege of climbing to the roof of a two-story building where they were able to watch the entire proceedings.

When the parade was over, however, they discovered to their dismay that someone had taken away the ladder on which they had reached their vantage spot on the roof.

Finally, after a 45-minute wait, another enterprising person brought along a ladder of his own. However, he charged them $1 each to climb down again.

Shrewdness and sharpness are commendable traits provided one does not take advantage of the rights of others, especially when they are in a predicament.

A safe, sane and truly divine standard to follow in all your business dealings is to charge or pay the same price that you yourself would expect, no matter on which end of the ladder you happen to be!

Whatever you wish that men would do to you, do so to them; for this is the law and the prophets. (Mt. 7:12)

Grant, Lord, that I may keep in mind the rights of others while providing for my own personal needs.

Why Teaching Is Worthwhile

"To get the confidence of the boys and girls in the classroom, to feel that one has a part in molding the citizens of our country — these two facts alone make a teacher's life worthwhile."

This is how Gertrude Geraghty felt after teaching for over 30 years in the public schools of Memphis.

This devoted woman spelled out the type of dedication needed in the classroom:

"The teacher's whole soul must be bent on making her pupils come alive. She must be a master salesman and competition is keen.

"To prod the lazy, to lure the difficult, to encourage the slow, and to guide them all, she must possess the charm of a Cleopatra, the wiles of a Machiavelli, the patience of Job, the gentleness of St. Francis, and the wisdom of Solomon."

Even though your vocation in life is not that of a teacher, do your part to encourage those with high ideals and competence to dedicate themselves in Christ's name to this noble profession.

Those who are wise shall shine like the brightness of the firmament; and those who turn many to righteousness, like the stars for ever and ever. (Dan. 12:3)

Bless in a special way, Divine Teacher, all who undertake the career of a teacher.

Passing Resolutions Not Enough

Members of a worthwhile organization were shocked recently when their president read them a list of 46 resolutions they had passed at meetings during the year. No action had been taken on any of them.

It was a polite but effective reminder that little if anything is settled by merely "passing resolutions," however excellent they may be.

For constructive action, good ideas must, of course, be rooted in sound principles. But unless they are backed up by more than talk, they will never be more than high-sounding principles "on the shelf," waiting to be translated into performance.

For every minute you spend talking about how the world should be improved, devote at least another 20 minutes to practical ways and means of really doing what you advocate.

You can make a valuable contribution as a Christ bearer by putting your good ideas into daily practice. That is the recommendation of the Lord Himself.

Not every one who says to Me, "Lord, Lord," shall enter the kingdom of heaven, but he who does the will of My Father who is in heaven. (Mt. 7:21)

Lord Jesus, may I be a "doer" of the Father's will rather than only a "talker."

What Can I Do?

When you consider the vastness of world problems, you may ask yourself, "What can I possibly do about any of them?"

The very fact that you conscientiously ask yourself that question means that you are on the road to providing your own part of the answer.

Take even a small step towards improving your surroundings and be prepared for a surprise. You will be startled at how quickly God opens doors for you when you are fired by hope, not blanketed by despair.

These few tips may help you:

▓ Remember that the rebuilding of a good world starts with you as much as it does with anybody.

▓ Be a doer, not a complainer. Cynics, defeatists and other "nay-sayers" serve little purpose by grumbling from the sidelines.

▓ In short, replace a shout of "Why doesn't somebody do something?" with the calm, determined question, "What can I do?"

Blessed rather are those who hear the word of God and keep it! (Lk. 11:28)

Inspire me, Spirit of Wisdom, to grapple with problems, not merely talk about them.

Blind Child Saves Family

A nine-year-old blind girl saved her family when their house caught fire.

When the child was awakened by the smell of smoke in her bedroom, she was sure she could feel her way to safety, but was worried about her mother and 10-year-old brother, who were not used to groping in the dark.

The blind youngster quickly hurried to their bedrooms. She found them groggy from the smoke but was able to lead them from the burning building.

No matter how limited your ability or circumstances may be, you can render an important and needed contribution to life.

If you are motivated by a strong desire to be of service to others, you are bound to find constructive outlets for your inner power.

Deepen your love for God and others, and you will find many ways of translating it into practical application.

Every one helps his neighbor, and says to his brother, "Take courage!" (Is. 41:6)

Inspire me, Holy Spirit, to be alert to the physical and spiritual needs of others.

Put Love Where There Is No Love

The town of Accord, N.Y., got its significant name as a result of the resourcefulness of a postal clerk about 200 years ago.

The first settlers of the village in the late 1700s wrangled constantly about a name for their town.

One irate citizen finally took the matter into his own hands and wrote the Postmaster General, suggesting that, because of all the squabbling the new community should be labeled "Discord."

A clerk in the department delegated to work out a practical solution finally hit on one that pleased everybody. He suggested that the town be called "Accord."

One person can do much to replace disagreement with harmony in the home, at work or any place.

You can be a peacemaker and pour oil on troubled waters by taking the trouble and initiative to bring Christ's love into the midst of dissension.

Blessed are the peacemakers for they shall be called children of God. (Mt. 5:9)

Permit me to be a generous instrument of Your peace, Lord.

Sick Baby Gets Blood From Paris

A 10-day-old baby, critically ill with a rare blood ailment in a Long Island hospital, received a pint of blood from Paris.

The donor read an appeal for the A-positive blood in a French newspaper.

When he contacted the American embassy to offer his blood, the staff quickly accepted and made arrangements to have it flown to New York. The special type blood was picked up at Kennedy Airport and immediately taken to the hospital.

An example like this is heartening at a time when many seem to be quite careless about the fate of their fellow human beings all over the world.

Its simplicity is a forceful and hopeful reminder that human beings, despite human weakness, were given a divine inclination to be solicitous about their fellow human beings.

You will deepen your interest in humanity if you do everything you can to develop the habit of seeing God's holy image in every human being.

As you did it to one of the least of these My brethren, you did it to Me. (Mt. 25:40)

Imbue me with a deep and practical love for suffering humanity, Crucified Savior.

Auto Can't Run on Looks

A Texas motorist was rudely awakened when he tried to drive to work in his car. The vehicle looked perfectly normal when he climbed into it. But he soon found out that the carburetor, battery, generator, fan belt, fuel pump, oil filter, radiator cap and distributor were missing.

In addition to these essentials the thief had also made off with the cigarette lighter, clock, ash tray, rear view mirror, arm rests, floor mats, part of the antenna and the knobs off the radio.

Appearances can be most deceiving. It is easy to conclude that something is good, true or beautiful if we judge only what meets the eye. It is human to overemphasize the superficial — to confuse incidentals with essentials.

God expects us to be alert, not gullible. Investigate beneath the surface and avoid being taken in by appearances.

Do not judge by appearances, but judge with right judgment. (Jn. 7:24)

Lord who can neither deceive nor be deceived, help me to uphold truth and not judge by appearances.

Tot Saves Aunt

A two-year-old girl with a liking for telephones helped save her aunt who had collapsed with a stroke.

The two were alone when the woman suffered the attack. Shortly afterwards, the little girl picked up the receiver and dialed the operator with a sobbing message that her aunt was sick.

The operator traced the message and informed the police. They administered oxygen to the woman. She regained consciousness and was later reported in good condition.

The girl's mother said that her daughter had often played with a toy telephone and had been allowed on occasion to dial numbers on the real phone.

The resourcefulness of this little one underscores the powers instilled in children by their Creator. If she had not been encouraged to use her talent, the result might have been far different.

Praise and promote reasonable initiative in children. They will happily surprise you if you do.

See that you do not despise one of these little ones; for I tell you that in heaven their angels always behold the face of My Father who is in heaven. (Mt. 18:10)

Enable me to do all I can, Divine Child of Nazareth, to channel the energies of young people toward good.

Man Eludes Death Three Times

Death pursued a man three times in Chattanooga, Tenn., but left him unscratched.

To begin with, his car stalled at a grade crossing just as a freight train came roaring toward him. He managed to get out of the vehicle seconds before the locomotive plowed into it.

The impact of the collision sent the auto reeling towards the bewildered man. Once more he jumped out of danger as the wrecked car crashed into a railroad signal-crossing pole.

The pole was slammed so hard that it broke in half and toppled to the ground immediately behind the fleeing man.

You may never experience such a triple brush with death. But even those who lead a comparatively quiet existence need an occasional reminder that they have no lease on life.

Cram as much good as you can into your life and no matter when you are called, you will go with full hands before the judgment seat.

Be faithful unto death, and I will give you the crown of life . . . He who conquers shall not be hurt by the second death. (Rev. 2:10,11)

Keep me constantly aware, loving and merciful Father, that the longest life is all too short to prepare for death.

Make 'Perseverance' Your By-Word

"Without perseverance," advises an old Welsh proverb, "talent is a barren bed."

The great people of history set high goals for themselves and remained in the thick of the fight until they achieved their purpose.

The dictionary defines "persevere" as "persisting in any enterprise undertaken, in spite of counter influences and opposition."

It comes from the Latin word "per," meaning "through," and "severus," meaning "strict" or "difficult."

Samuel Johnson had this to say about this admirable quality, "Great works are performed, not by strength, but by perseverance."

While it is true that we may persevere in evil as well as in good, try to use your talents, few or many, to the best of your ability, and leave the rest to God.

In these days where personal comfort is so much regarded, resolve to be different by perseverance in deeds that are helpful to others and pleasing to your Maker.

Who endures to the end will be saved. (Mk. 13:13)

Grant me Your grace, most strong God, to be persevering in good.

'I Had to Save My Brother'

"I had to save my brother" was the simple explanation given by a young teenager after rescuing his two-year-old brother from drowning in a 20-foot well in Smithton, Pa.

The youngster had fallen into the well while playing. He screamed for help as he splashed about in four feet of water at the bottom. But, since the well was only 20 inches in diameter, and too narrow for a man to climb down, the 13-year-old boy volunteered. It was not an easy undertaking. Twice the little fellow slipped out of his brother's grip and fell back into the water.

When the two boys were finally pulled out, the older one modestly refused all compliments by saying: "That was my brother down there. I knew I had to get him out some way."

Try to comprehend the tremendous meaning of the words of the "Our Father" and you will look beyond your own family circle, and see in every person your sister or brother, especially when they are in need.

> **God is not so unjust as to overlook your work and the love which you showed for His sake in serving the saints. (Heb. 6:10)**

> *Thanks, Father-God, for the privilege of being Your child and brother or sister to every human being.*

Teenager Aids Hospital

It was a 15-year-old girl who made the most significant contribution to a fund-raising drive for a children's hospital in Memphis. Despite the fact that she had been an invalid all her life, the teenager was able to raise over a thousand dollars.

The young woman was born with amyatonia, a rare disease that leaves its sufferers with almost complete lack of muscular control. This did not prevent her from working from her wheelchair for two summers. She sold lemonade for the benefit of children she considered less fortunate than herself.

Many persons with handicaps show great determination to reach out to the world in a positive manner. Their quiet heroism amid the challenges of life should inspire others to take a second look at just how they are using their God-given abilities.

Keep in mind always that the Lord will ask us whether we used our talents for the good of others, or buried them.

Well done, good and faithful servant; you have been faithful over a little, I will set you over much; enter into the joy of your master. (Mt. 25:21)

Help me realize, just and loving Judge, that my concern should be more for the good I don't do, than for my mistakes.

Give Credit Where It Is Due

Two men were discussing their respective accomplishments, and during the conversation one of them proudly announced: "Everything I am I owe to myself. I'm a self-made man!"

It is symptomatic of a lack of insight when we make the mistake of thinking we are "self-made." Our bodies and brains we receive from God through our parents. Our knowledge we acquire from those who have gone before us.

Many of our skills depend upon our physical make-up. Our tastes and appreciations have come to us through our association with those who love the finer things.

Even that very precious possession, our conscience, will be affected for good or ill according to the training we receive. It is not a mysterious something requiring no guidance or training.

So there it is: our bodies, temperaments, brains we receive at birth. Other people pass on to us accumulated culture. We know right from wrong largely because we have been told which is which.

Why, then, should we flatter ourselves that everything we have and are is our own masterpiece? Let's give credit where it is due.

What have you that you did not receive? If then you received it, why do you boast as if it were not a gift? (1 Cor. 4:7)

Lord, let me be humbly grateful for all You have given me.

The Fear of Inconvenience

A prominent businessman was in a serious automobile accident several years ago. It was a head-on collision, and both cars rolled over. Several people were seriously injured and needed immediate attention.

The man crawled out of the wreckage and discovered that his head was covered with blood.

He saw a car coming and waved frantically for help. The car slowed down, but as it pulled alongside him he heard a voice say: "Don't stop. We may have to testify in court." The car picked up speed and disappeared down the road.

The natural instinct of these people was to help. But on second thought, the fear of becoming involved was stronger. They didn't want to be inconvenienced, so they drove off, perhaps leaving someone to die.

If you wish to be a Christ-bearer, you must expect to be inconvenienced — to suffer for the sake of others. But if you do, the Lord will bless your effort and you will find that there is more joy in it than suffering.

A man was going down from Jerusalem to Jericho, and he fell among robbers who stripped him and beat him, and departed, leaving him half dead . . . But a Samaritan, as he journeyed, came to where he was, and when he saw him he had compassion. (Lk. 10:30,33)

Merciful Savior, let me spend and be spent for others in a spirit of compassion.

Put the Man Right

An overworked businessman came home one night, hoping to read the evening paper in peace and quiet. But his six-year-old son wanted attention.

Tearing into small pieces a part of the paper which had a map of the world on one side of it and the picture of a man on the other, the father gave it to his son and told him to put the map back together again.

In 10 minutes his son returned, the task completed. Since the boy had no idea of geography, the businessman wondered how he had done so well so quickly.

"All I did," said the boy, "was to put the man right. When I did that, the world came out right."

The big battle of our day is over human beings — the worth of human beings. It is a battle for humanity's soul.

Are you doing as much to reach everyone with the truth of their divine origin as are those who deny God and are striving to eliminate all knowledge of Him from the face of the earth?

We are not contending against flesh and blood, but against the principalities, against the powers, against the world rulers of this present darkness. (Eph. 6:12)

Lord, help me to do my part in the battle for the soul of humanity.

The Chicken Who Never Got There

A chicken crossing a road in North Carolina caused a great deal of trouble.

It began when the chicken dashed out on the road in front of a fast-moving car. The driver jammed on his brakes to avoid hitting the fowl.

The car behind tried to swerve to the side of the road but banged into the first auto, which in turn, squashed the chicken. Meanwhile, a third vehicle, a tank truck, clipped the first two cars and climbed an embankment, trying to avoid a collision.

Damages amounted to thousands of dollars — and one squashed chicken.

Far-reaching harm may be the result of even slightly imprudent actions. God expects us to use good judgment in meeting modern problems.

Avoid overcaution, but at the same time beware of recklessness, lest, inadvertently, you cause injury to others.

Be wise as serpents and innocent as doves. (Mt. 10:16)

Grant that I may be both daring and restrained in furthering Your cause, Jesus.

Laws, Taxes and Insurance

In asking for more time to make payments to her creditors, one Cleveland shop owner wrote:

"In reply to your request to send a check, I wish to inform you the present condition of my bank account makes it almost impossible . . . due to federal laws, state laws, county laws, city laws, corporation laws, liquor laws, mother-in-laws, brother-in-laws, sister-in-laws and outlaws.

". . . I am expected to pay a business tax, school tax, gas tax, carpet tax, income tax, furniture tax and excise tax. Even my brains are taxed.

"I must get a business license, car license, hunting license, truck license, marriage and dog licenses.

"I am required to carry life insurance, property insurance, liability insurance, burglar insurance, unemployment insurance, accident insurance, earthquake insurance, tornado, old age and fire insurance."

Take care not to get so submerged in what protects your material well-being that you overlook the needs of your immortal soul.

Set your minds on things that are above, not on things that are on earth. For you have died, and your life is hid with Christ in God. (Col. 3:2-3)

Keep me mindful of eternal goals, Lord, while I care for temporal needs.

Older People Want to Serve

If you had been born in the Roman Empire you would have had a life expectancy of 23 years.

Even a century ago in New England the average person could count on about 40 years. By 1900 it had risen to 47. Today a newborn infant can have some assurance of reaching more than 70 years.

The lengthening span of our earthly life accounts for the increasing number of older persons in our society.

The growing proportion of senior citizens in our country can be a great blessing. Their seasoned experience has brought them a maturity and wisdom that is desperately needed.

The greatest love and respect you can show to aging persons is to give them opportunities to make constructive use of their God-given powers.

Do whatever you can to find useful employment for older persons. Show them they are both wanted and needed.

Rise up before the hoary head, and honor the face of the old. (Lev. 19:32)

Alert us to the needs of our elders, Creator, and enable us to help them lead lives of dignity and usefulness.

Paid in Full

The white-haired surgeon smiled down at the frail old lady. "You've done it, Miss Lucy! You can go home tomorrow."

"I didn't do it, Doctor," Miss Lucy answered. "It was your skill, your great kindness!" She hesitated, and then went on. "Your bills are always so small, Doctor, and I even have to remind you to send them. I haven't a great deal, but I want to pay. Remember that, please, and let me know what I owe you."

The surgeon nodded briskly. "I won't forget. You'll hear from me." Two days later Miss Lucy received her bill. The figure was shockingly large. But across the bottom of the invoice, in the doctor's firm hand, were the words: "Paid in full with a gracious personality."

Every day we have numerous opportunities of being generous, especially to those in need. We should be generous not only with money, but with our time and talent. There are many people who can best be helped by a loving consideration for them and their problems.

God loves a cheerful giver. (2 Cor. 9:7)

Lord, teach me to be generous with the blessings You have given me.

Inherits Fortune Despite Everyone

A patient had the last laugh on a Czech doctor who had tried to cure him of the obsession that he was about to inherit a fortune.

For many months the man persisted in the "ridiculous notion" that a mysterious "American uncle" would leave him a large sum of money.

After undergoing a series of treatments for his hallucinations, he was released from the hospital. The very next day he received a telegram notifying him that a cousin had died in the United States, leaving him $70,000.

While such bountiful dreams rarely come true, don't dismiss as visionary the spiritual rewards that can be yours both here and hereafter if your life is always motivated by a deep faith, hope and charity.

Centuries ago Isaiah urged the Jewish people to lift their sights and look far ahead to the enduring rewards of eternity.

From of old no one has heard or perceived by the ear, no eye has seen a God besides You, who works for those who wait for Him. (Is. 64:4)

Grant me, Holy Spirit, the perseverance to merit the eternal legacy You promise to those who are loyal to You.

Work Can Be a Pleasure

"Labor is a pleasure in itself," is an ancient maxim that many moderns would regard with jaundiced eye. The press of hard facts, however, forces upon us sooner or later the awareness that we never find true fulfillment without hard and rewarding work.

Before the coming of Christ, Vergil, the Roman poet, said: "Labor conquers all things." His comment was echoed by that of Horace: "Life gives nothing to man without labor."

The early Christians sanctified, or made holy, all work in the home, at study, in the fields, shops and arts. They knew that their efforts, however insignificant, had a part to play in rebuilding the earth according to God's design for human happiness in time and eternity.

See in each day's tasks a fresh opportunity to participate in the creative work of God who made the world. Armed with this positive viewpoint, you will have discovered the deepest joy of labor.

Come to Me, all who labor and are heavy laden, and I will give you rest. (Mt. 11:28)

Thank you, Creator, for allowing me to be Your co-worker in renewing the face of the earth.

The High Price of Ingratitude

Those who take their blessings for granted often lose them when least expected.

Several residents in a Connecticut town who had been receiving free firewood for 10 years discovered this to their surprise and regret.

The local tree department had been giving away wood from storm-damaged and disease-stricken trees but found that this service was far from appreciated.

Recipients of the free wood complained that it didn't arrive cut in the correct lengths or wasn't stacked neatly in their cellars. The tree department stopped giving away firewood.

Ingratitude is at the bottom of many of the problems that beset the world. Those who are unthankful not only hurt themselves but withhold the appreciation due others. Little wonder that Shakespeare said "Ingratitude! thou marbleheaded fiend."

Take a few moments each day to thank God for the many blessings that come your way. You will be the better for it if you do — and others will, too!

Remember the Lord our God all your days. (Tobit 4:5)

Thank you, heavenly Father, for all that I am and ever hope to be.

Chickens Killed by Fear

The sight of a marauding owl pushed the panic button for 3,000 little chicks in Prairieville, La. They piled up in a corner of the chicken house and proceeded to smother themselves.

After the poultryman had shot the owl, he found that only two of the four-week-old chicks had been killed by the bird. Fear had proved the undoing of all the rest.

Proper concern for impending danger is only right, but do not allow yourself to be stampeded into unreasoning fear.

The following points may help:

■ You can't expect to cope with any danger unless you know something about it.

■ Work hard to help your fellow men and women achieve the dignity and equal opportunity they deserve, and let out dangerous situations by the back door.

■ Remember that God is a loving parent, Who can bring good out of the worst catastrophes.

Fear not, little flock, for it is your Father's good pleasure to give you the kingdom. (Lk. 12:32)

Never let crippling fear prevent my carrying out the Father's will, Jesus.

Jungle Odyssey Lasts 19 Days

Lost for nearly three weeks in the tangled horror of Brazil's Mato Grosso jungle, a bush pilot and a travelling salesman finally reached safety.

The two men were flying for a contracting company when strong winds blew them off course. Without any reference points over the matted green expanse, they ran out of gas and had to crash-land.

Equipped with a cheese and a salami sandwich, 10 biscuits, pistol and fishing line, they set out in the direction where they thought rescue more likely. For 19 broiling days and shivering nights they slogged through swamp and jungle before reaching a point where a plane spotted their smoke signal.

The pilot had lost 40 pounds and the salesman was in a state of fever and delirium as a Brazilian Air Force rescue craft flew them back to civilization.

You don't have to fly over the jungle to lose your bearings in life. Keep the compass of God's commandments with you for a safe flight to eternity.

Blessed are those whose way is blameless, who walk in the law of the Lord! (Ps. 119:1)

Never permit me, O Lord, to lose my direction or run out of gas in spreading afar Your law of love.

Child Lives Despite Long Fall

A six-year-old girl proved to be about the most durable child in San Francisco history.

Little Dorothy tumbled out of a third-story apartment house window, struck a planter box on the floor below, landed on a six-foot wooden fence and finally fell into a small concrete enclosure.

The doctor summoned to treat the youngster was astonished to find that, apart from a bruised eye and a scratched hip, she was none the worse for her big tumble.

"It's amazing," the doctor commented. "No, it's more than that . . . it's miraculous."

It is a never-ending source of wonder that Providence watches over all of us, young and old alike.

Pause a few moments each day in reflection and prayer. Count the many blessings of body and soul that you personally enjoy and for which you are entirely dependent upon a loving God.

The more you realize the generosity of the Lord to you, the more inclined you will be to show a similar solicitude for others.

Fear not; you are of more value than many sparrows. (Lk. 12:7)

Thank you, bountiful Lord, for the countless blessings You send to each of us daily.

A Stylish Getaway Fails

A seemingly model prisoner made a walking escape from an honor farm in California. Being a Texan, he felt the need of a horse.

Not only did he rent a horse with his spending money, but he equipped himself with a large black sombrero, spurs and chaps.

Things went well until the escapee's hat blew off. As he dismounted to recover it, the animal ran away. He rented a second mount but a highway patrolman stopped him while he was riding in this unusual style along a freeway.

"He said he didn't know where he was going," the patrolman related. "He just wanted to get someplace else."

Most people who don't know where they're going seldom get anywhere. Use as much creativeness and energy in finding keys to world problems as others do in creating them. Then you can be sure that God will show you where you are going — and see that you get there.

I do not run aimlessly, I do not box as one beating the air. (1 Cor. 9:26)

Make me know where I am headed, Father, and help others along the same way.

To Love One's Enemies

Speaking well of those who disliked him was one of Gen. Robert E. Lee's outstanding qualities.

When he paid generous tribute to the ability of a certain colleague, a fellow officer remarked:

"General, how can you speak so highly of one of our bitterest enemies, a man who never misses an opportunity to malign you?"

"My friend," Lee replied, "the President asked my opinion of him, not his opinion of me."

By cultivating the habit of thinking and speaking well of others, regardless of their attitude towards you, you will make an investment that will bear rich dividends for time and eternity.

Paradoxically enough you will bring peace to yourself, and to others as well as to a world much in need of every bit of peace that you and others like you can provide.

It is a sign of strength rather than weakness to follow this pattern, Christ's pattern, of thinking and speaking well of others.

Love your enemies and pray for those who persecute you so that you may be children of your Father who is in heaven. (Mt. 5:44-45)

Help me, gentle Master, to focus attention on the good qualities of those who dislike me.

Soft Drink Proves Expensive

An unsuspecting soul paid the equivalent of $35 for a soft drink in an Arkansas school. When the day's proceeds from the dispensing machine were counted, it was discovered that a 1916 D Mercury dime lay among the dozens of other dimes. The employee who found it, a coin collector, immediately recognized its value.

The odds against stumbling upon a rare coin are exceedingly high. However, there are many things of real worth we encounter each day and allow to pass by unnoticed.

Among these valuable opportunities are:

■ The cheery greeting we owe everyone we meet. More often than not it will raise the spirits of those who very much need it.

■ The stand we ought to take for truth, honesty and decency.

Go on a treasure hunt today for chances to serve God by an outgoing consideration for others.

You shall not oppress your neighbor . . . You shall not hate your brother. (Lev. 19:13,17)

Make me an expert, O Lord, in transforming the raw material of daily living into a joy for myself and others.

Baby Saves Family

The loud crying of a six-week-old baby saved her sleeping parents, a sister and two brothers from silent death, when coal gas engulfed their apartment in Plainfield, N.J.

When the 27-year-old father was awakened by the infant's cries, he found his wife unconscious. He quickly opened the windows; revived her and then carried the baby and other three children to safety.

Whether young or old, in low position or high, you can fulfill a Christ-like mission by making your voice heard especially when others are threatened by deadly evils of which they are unaware.

You can do something, however small, to right what is wrong or to prevent a repetition of misfortune. Complaining or criticizing has some value, but it is always "better to light one candle than to curse the darkness."

You will be more alert to dangers if you are motivated by a deep love of others for the love of God.

Who does the will of God abides for ever. (1 Jn. 2:17)

Help me to be of service to others in every way possible, Divine Master.

Three Years to Pay for a Newspaper

It took one man three years to pay for a daily paper he picked up in a newsstand in London.

"I'll be right back" were the last words the news dealer heard from him until the repentant individual returned recently with an apology and the money for the paper he had taken from his stand a few years before.

The man sheepishly explained that he had been arrested and had spent the intervening 36 months in jail for non-payment of other debts.

Weak human nature often causes us to falter and fail in our obligations to others.

However, there is always hope because a sense of right and wrong lingers in the heart of every person. Faint as it may seem at times, this voice of conscience can never be completely extinguished.

Live more and more by the standards of a good conscience and you will grow in the enjoyment of the divine peace of heart, mind and soul, which God wishes all to share.

Who pursues righteousness and kindness will find life and honor. (Prov. 21:21)

Let my life be guided by Your changeless truths, Lord God.

What's Your Goal?

Riding an outboard motor for 232 consecutive hours was the record set by a 55-year-old retired motel operator in Florida.

After spending nearly 10 sleepless days circling a lake, the tenacious man finally stumbled off to bed, after admitting that he had suffered hallucinations at times while putt-putting around.

The desire to outstrip others leads human beings to a whole variety of feats from climbing mountains to being the best dressed to having the lowest golf score or to sitting on a flag pole.

But the price is never light and the result never very satisfying compared to the tremendous amount of thought, time, energy and downright suffering that must be devoted to achieving such goals.

People certainly need a challenge in life. God made us that way. But we get our truest sense of fulfillment when we strive for worthwhile goals that benefit everyone rather than those centered on self-glory.

Who sows to the Spirit will from the Spirit reap eternal life. (Gal. 6:8)

God, help me to seek the good of all rather than my own selfish whims.

Marriage: More Than a Ring

A wedding ring lost for close to 60 years turned up just where it disappeared — in the backyard of the woman who owned it.

The ring was found by a daughter-in-law, who was digging in a tulip patch. Still legible was the inscription: "M.K. to A.K., 1899."

Whatever its value, though, as the symbol of married love, a ring can only be the outward sign of inward loyalty and devotion. It is of incidental worth in comparison with the priceless treasure of a happy marriage, of which God Himself is the author.

Do everything in your power to help husbands and wives who manage to keep their rings but who fail to guard and cherish the holy bond of matrimony.

A slight effort on your part may save a marriage that is weakening. Build up in husbands and wives the mutual, unselfish love that means infinitely more to marriage than a carload of wedding rings. You will be blessed by God and others if you do.

Let marriage be held in honor among all, and let the marriage bed be undefiled. (Heb. 13:4)

Smile, O Lord, upon all who work to make a success of their married life in the face of all obstacles.

Daring Needs Restraint

Two 12-year-old boys alarmed onlookers in Norfolk, Va., who watched them drift down the 40-foot deep Elizabeth River on a makeshift raft.

The Coast Guard finally rescued them as they were floating toward the open ocean in their unseaworthy craft.

Young people are blessed with a daring and adventurous spirit. But their enthusiasm and resourcefulness must be properly directed or channeled. At the same time great care must be taken not to suppress or stifle the potential greatness of boys and girls by restraining them too much.

The Lord Himself encouraged His apostles to "launch out into the deep" as "fishers of men." But at the same time He stressed that they should be firmly rooted in divine truth and love.

Develop in youth the ability to be daring without ever being foolish or reckless.

Put out into the deep and let down your nets for a catch. (Lk. 5:4)

Thanks to You, Divine Redeemer, for encouraging me to be daring in Your cause.

Windfall for Children

A 70-year-old toymaker gave his toy shop to the children of Denmark.

His "House of Toys," one of the biggest in the world, was started more than 125 years earlier by his family. It was a favorite haunt of fairy-tale writer Hans Christian Anderson as well as hundreds of thousands of enchanted youngsters who romped through the five-story toyland.

In announcing that the toy store would be placed in trust for needy youngsters, the owner said:

"We earned all our money from children, so it comes quite naturally to us to give the money back to the children, especially to those who have never had the joy that toys may give."

God blesses those who show gratitude. It is a quality that all of us would do well to cultivate and apply in our workaday world. In the home, school, shop, office, and in every other setting, even a slight expression of gratefulness adds a divine touch that warms and inspires.

Let the children come to Me, and do not hinder them; for to such belongs the kingdom of God . . . whoever does not receive the kingdom of God like a child shall not enter it. (Lk. 18:16-17)

May You be blessed, Lord of heaven and earth, for that childlike joy which comes from You alone.

Balloon Changes a Boy's Life

A blue balloon found in a swamp lifted a 10-year-old boy into a new and dazzling world.

It all started when merchants in Harrisburg, Pa., let loose 864 gas-filled balloons to advertise the opening of a shopping center. Each contained a gift certificate.

The youngster found one of the balloons in a swamp in Milford, Conn., and wrote to the merchants.

They decided to send him a gift. When they phoned to tell him, the lad's mother said that he was suffering from a serious speech impediment, and that both parents had to work to support their four children.

So, instead of a little gift, he received a bicycle, pup tent, clothes, toys and a trip to Harrisburg, Pa., where he was made an honorary citizen.

A chance happening often brings out the compassion that God expects of us towards others in need.

But don't wait for a balloon or an angel out of the blue to inspire you to help those who require it most. Lift up your eyes and do what you can.

When He saw the crowds, He had compassion for them, because they were harassed and helpless, like sheep without a shepherd. (Mt. 9:36)

Make me a self-starter, Compassionate Lord, in finding ways to bring Your love to my sisters and brothers.

He Looked Up and Saved a Life

The sight of a small child teetering on a third-story window ledge greeted a Brooklyn sanitation worker as he looked up.

Instantly he began the 30-foot run towards the 2-year-old child and arrived just in time to break his fall. They both tumbled into a large trash container.

The child suffered only minor injuries and his benefactor was unhurt.

A split second's hesitation on the part of this brave city employee could have been fatal to the little one. He looked up, he made his decision — and he acted.

In many less dramatic but still important ways, God gives us the vision of a job to be done, a wrong to be righted. He also gives us the resources to do something about it, if we will only let Him.

Seize today's opportunity to do good today, and tomorrow will take care of itself.

At the acceptable time I have listened to you, and helped you on the day of salvation. (2 Cor. 6:2)

Prompt me with Your grace, Lord, to be alert for every chance to do good.

Love of Children Essential for Teacher

"You must like children!" This is essential for a good teacher, John B. Smith, one-time superintendent of schools in Greenwich, Conn., impressed on a group of new teachers at the beginning of the school year.

The first question a teacher should ask, Smith said, is: "Do I really like children? Do I honestly like to work with them . . .? We have to love them to be in the business."

The educator suggested that the teachers also ask themselves: "Am I friendly?" Then he added: "You have to be friendly to your fellow teachers and to the children, who can sense when you are not."

Competence is needed, to be sure, for a good homemaker, laborer, doctor, scriptwriter or legislator, as well as for a teacher. But for one and all, the dominant quality should be love of people.

You can be an instrument of Christ Himself in transmitting some of His divine love into the lives of young and old alike. God sends it to them through you!

Love is the fulfilling of the law. (Rom. 13:10)

Teach me, Jesus, to love others as You love me.

One Candle Lights Another

"When people growl about their crooked politicians, I ask them if they voted last time. If a worker screams about a strike, I ask how active he or she is in their union. You would be surprised at the excuses and stammering."

This brief message was sent by a woman in Baltimore who picked up the Christopher motto of "lighting a candle instead of cursing the darkness."

Shortly after we published her story, a suburban woman wrote, "The lady in Maryland made me sit up and take notice."

She said her husband, a union member, never went to a meeting. She began urging him to go and see what was happening.

When he found only a handful present, he was so shocked by the negligence of good members that he started to build up attendance. After months of hard work, he had nearly a 100 percent turnout.

As one woman changed a union, so can you, with God's help, do something to change the world.

Who looks into the perfect law, the law of liberty, and perseveres, being no hearer that forgets but a doer that acts, he shall be blessed. (Jas. 1:25)

Enable me, Lord, to reach out to a world in great need of Your love and truth.

Punishment Fits the Crime

A quick-witted coed in Michigan decided it was only right to make "the punishment fit the crime." Receiving a ticket for making an illegal turn at an intersection, she made up her mind to help other motorists profit by her mistake.

She sent the money to the judge, and attached the following note:

"I thought you might be interested to know that I earned the money for the fine by writing safety slogans for a Detroit radio station."

The impressed magistrate suspended sentence.

Few people get the opportunity to make up for their transgressions, large and small, by such an appropriate means. Fewer still may have the inclination. But God blesses those who do.

There is something winning about the humility and good sense of those who meet their shortcomings head-on and root them out.

Take a good hard look at yourself and improve the world by doing something about what you see.

> **First take the log out of your own eye, and then you will see clearly to take out the speck that is in your brother's eye. (Lk. 6:42)**

Spirit of Wisdom, help us to know ourselves as You know us.

Think Things Through

School examinations in France produced a few answers that were anything but pearls of wisdom.

Here are some samples:

"The highest form of animal life is the giraffe."

"To prevent forest fires, trees should be planted in the shade."

"Hedgehogs and swallows are the animals who help gardeners eat the insects."

"The moon is believed to be inhabited because of the light that comes from there."

"Living things found in polar places include lichen, moss, penguins and explorers."

Scrambled thinking may be a bit amusing, but it is no laughing matter if young people are continually allowed to shirk their responsibility to think clearly and logically.

God endows each of us with intelligence. He expects us to develop it and put it to good use, not to abuse it by neglect or faulty thinking.

Happy is the man who finds wisdom, and the man who gets understanding, for the gain from it is better than gain from silver and its profit better than gold. (Pr. 3:13-14)

Holy Spirit, enable me to express my gratitude for Your gift of intelligence.

Do You Know Yourself?

Paddling and sailing an 18-foot folding boat for 5,629 miles from Buenos Aires to Miami proved to be a challenging nine-month adventure for a 48-year-old Argentine.

For one period of seven days his small open craft, called "Faith, Love and Perseverance," never touched shore. He had neither compass nor radio. He steered by the stars and depended on the prevailing winds and currents.

He explained how the long trip had helped put life in perspective: "When you are alone at sea you understand the valor, the pain and the happiness of the human being."

Few people could or would take such an expedition. But there are many ways you can enter into yourself and rediscover what you are and why you were created by God.

Set aside a few minutes each day for prayerful meditation and you will find increased happiness in being a human being.

Man shall not live by bread alone but by every word that proceeds from the mouth of God. (Mt. 4:4)

Father, thank you for creating me in Your holy image.

Goes to Jail to Get a Meal

A hungry man held up a cab in Manhattan so that he would be arrested and get a much-needed meal in jail.

When the police seized the half-hearted robber, he offered no resistance. They found two pennies in his pocket.

"I did this," the defendant admitted frankly in court, "because I was hungry. I didn't want to do anything bad. I had to do something before I might hurt someone."

Then, with head lowered, he added, "Judge, do you know what it is to be hungry and not to have eaten in two days?"

Even a brief encounter with the bite of hunger would make all of us more sympathetic to those who are poorly fed in our midst, and to the hundreds of millions over the earth who are on the verge of starvation.

Help them to have the daily bread God wishes them to have and you will likewise help them lead purposeful, law-abiding lives.

Share your bread with the hungry, and bring the homeless poor into your house. (Is. 58:7)

Show me, Divine Provider, how to give an abundance of food to those who suffer the gnawing pangs of hunger.

Canary's Death Results in Suit

A canary was scared to death by fireworks at a Fourth of July celebration in New Rochelle, N.Y. As a result, the owners of the pet won a settlement on their claim for the loss of the bird.

According to the owners, their canary had been "carefree and untroubled," a "sweet singer and a pet of incomparable worth" until the exploding fireworks in the park across the street got it so wildly agitated that it died of a heart attack.

The manufacturer of the fireworks offered to relieve the city of all responsibility and paid the cost of the settlement in the interests of good will.

If we place such a high value on a canary, think what every human being must be worth in God's sight.

In these days, when the big battle is over the worth of human life, do your part to champion the eternal value of human life because human life is made in the image of our Creator.

> **Consider the ravens: they neither sow nor reap, they have neither storehouse nor barn, and yet God feeds them. Of how much more value are you than the birds! (Lk. 12:24)**

Father, remind us of our importance in Your sight and of Your compassionate care for all our needs.

The Weeds Took Over

A man in Ohio found out the hard way that it doesn't pay to raise dandelions.

A local ordinance prohibits residents from letting dandelions grow in such profusion that they take over a yard.

When this particular individual didn't take the ruling too seriously, he was given the alternative of paying a $25 fine or digging up all the dandelions within 10 days.

It is not easy to keep ahead of weeds by simply fighting them. However, a person who takes a positive approach and fills a garden with good plants finds that there is less room for weeds to flourish.

Apply this lesson to every phase of life and you will find that being for good is much more effective than merely being against evil.

God gives each of us both the ability and the grace to prevent and overcome evil in the world rather than sit idly by until it debases or submerges us.

Do not be overcome by evil, but overcome evil with good. (Rom. 12:21)

Teach me to restore the good, O Lord, rather than merely complain about evil.

Your Freedom Is God-Given

In 1751, 25 years before the signing of the Declaration of Independence, the Founding Fathers of the United States sent an order to England for the now-famous Liberty Bell.

In the same year (1751) when the Council of Philadelphia gave instructions for the casting of the bell, it specified that the following passage from the Holy Bible be inscribed in large letters on the bell:

"Proclaim liberty throughout all the land unto all the inhabitants thereof." (Lev. 25:10)

Millions of persons who visit Independence Hall in Philadelphia are given pause for reflection when they read this scriptural text on the bell. It reminds them that the early Americans were anxious from the very beginning to make this a nation under God, not one without Him.

Keep others aware of the intimate connection between God and liberty. Point out that those who would enslave people try to hide the fact that they derive their rights from God, and that no State can take them away.

Where the Spirit of the Lord is, there is freedom. (2 Cor. 3:17)

Thanks to You, Bountiful Father, for the precious gift of freedom.

Two Eyes Help Six to See

A single pair of eyes bequeathed to an eye bank makes is possible for six blind people to see again. This heartening fact was made known by a doctor who pioneered in eye research.

Surgical advances and new drugs have enabled experts to transplant the two healthy corneas (transparent coat of the eyeball) to replace damaged ones. At the same time the vitreous or jelly-like substance of the two sound organs can be inserted into four eyes suffering from blindness caused by detachment of the retina.

It is only when the affliction of blindness is brought to our attention that most of us appreciate God's incalculable gift of eyesight. It is the most noble of our five senses.

Try in every way to use your eyes in the manner for which they were intended. Look about you for chances to lighten the burdens of your fellow human beings. Your reward will be the joy of serving God in this life and seeing God face to face for all eternity.

What no eye has seen, nor ear heard, nor the heart . . . conceived what God has prepared for those who love Him, God has revealed to us through the Spirit. (1 Cor. 2:9-10)

Enlighten us, Lord, with insight into Your holy will.

Do It Right and Hear Music

A musical toothbrush invented by a man in Baltimore was once awarded a patent. The inventor explained that his device not only provides harmony but also encourages the proper brushing of teeth.

The right way, it seems, to clean one's teeth is to move the instrument up and down, thereby getting rid of food particles that lodge in the crevices. The all too common practice of brushing horizontally is considered ineffective.

The new musical brush will produce melodic strains only when it is worked up and down. Otherwise the user is greeted with a stony silence.

Whether or not musical brushes are the wave of the future, there is much to be said for the fact that harmony results only when we do things the right way. That is how God made us.

Obey the commandments, show as much concern for your neighbors' rights as for your own, help them in their need, and you will hear the music of a good conscience.

Hark, glad songs of victory in the tents of the righteous. (Ps. 118:15)

May we, O Lord God, find peace in carrying out Your will.

Heroism in Mid-Air

Dangling helplessly from a plane at the end of a line 3,200 feet in the air over Ontario, a student parachutist came within a few seconds of plummeting to death.

He was saved by the quick-thinking heroism of an instructor who slid down the line and opened the trapped man's parachute. His right arm had gotten tangled in the line and was tightly fastened against his body.

As the instructor reached the helpless victim and pulled the ripcord, the overstrained line snapped. Both landed safely.

One shudders to think, "What would I do?" in such a terrifying moment. Without more than seconds for reflection and the dangers so great, only someone with the highest respect for the value of a human life would attempt such a feat.

In many lesser ways you can show an effective regard for the God-given dignity of others.

You can take a stand for the human rights of all.

I trust in You, O Lord. I say, "You are my God." (Ps. 31:14)

Creator, in all I say and do show me how to build up respect for my fellow human beings.

Personalize Everything

Violinists enrich a symphony orchestra by the individual touch they bring into their playing.

If each one played exactly the same way, the effect would sound like the amplification of a single instrument, according to an acoustical scientist, Melville Clark, Jr.

"Of course, the violinists must play very closely together to produce good music," Clark added. "But they play just far enough apart, in pitch and timing, to achieve a richness, an aliveness, which they would not have if they were playing precisely alike."

Whether you are a homemaker, farmer, clerk, executive, or student, you have been entrusted by the Lord with an individuality of your own. It may seem insignificant to you, but through it you can add a touch of love and beauty to the world that is very much needed.

God wants you to personalize all you do while following faithfully the "notes" of His revealed law. The world will be the richer for it if you do.

Turn in the account of your stewardship, for you can no longer be steward. (Lk. 16:2)

Thank You, Holy Spirit, for giving me a personality of my own.

Anger Proves Costly

One little mouse nearly brought down the house in Baltimore. Here's how it happened.

An apartment owner was at his wit's end trying to catch the elusive creature that was disturbing his peace and quiet.

After every one of his attempts failed, he picked up his 12-gauge shotgun and aimed right for the mouse, letting go with both barrels.

He got results all right, but not the ones he was looking for. Not only had he blown out a wall of his apartment, but, to add insult to injury, the mouse escaped.

The final blow came when he was fined for "disturbing the peace, discharging firearms in the city, and possession of a deadly weapon."

In tackling any problem, take care lest you make a bad situation worse. Stick to a positive, constructive approach. Find the element of good and build on that. God will bless you if you make it your business to "build up," not "tear down."

Hate what is evil, hold fast to what is good . . . be aglow with the Spirit, serve the Lord. (Rom. 12:9,11)

Help me to be positive and constructive, Jesus, rather than negative and critical.

The Price Is Hard Work

Hitters are made, not born, according to Ted Williams, the former Boston Red Sox star and one of the outstanding batters in baseball history.

He admitted having some talent plus good eyesight but quickly added that it was "no better than that of a lot of other people."

He credited his batting success to hard work. "I could always hit," he said, "but that's because I worked at it. I was always the first kid at school in the morning waiting for the janitor to open up so that I could grab the bat."

Neither skill at sports nor any worthwhile undertaking is the result of wishful thinking. Results are usually in direct proportion to the amount of hard work put into any project.

The test of your sincerity in improving the world in which you live will be measured by the amount of time and effort you devote to that big task.

I was born and . . . have come into the world, to bear witness to the truth. (Jn. 18:37)

Help me imitate You, O Divine Savior, in working for the glory of the Father and the good of others.

Don't Stop Yourself

A Danish seaman, 43-year-old Vagn Astrup, fell unnoticed from his ship, the Norwegian tanker, Anne, about 14 miles before it reached the Panama Canal. He was not missed and the ship continued on to Cristobal.

The odds were certainly against the lone man's rescue in the midst of the Gulf of Mexico. But there was a slim chance, and Astrup knew that if he once gave up swimming, he was lost.

His faith and perseverance were not in vain. After he had been in the open sea for five hours, a passing ship spotted him and hurried to his rescue.

Those who strive to raise the level of modern life often feel discouraged in their fight for truth and decency. But this can be a ruse of the devil.

The surest way never to succeed is to give up. God blesses those who push on despite every obstacle. They gain in many ways. But those who stop themselves lose in every way.

I have fought the good fight, I have finished the race, I have kept the faith. (2 Tim. 4:7)

Inspire me, Spirit of Wisdom, to prove my faith in You by turning to You when tempted to discouragement.

Do It With Love

A husband once claimed that he could take cordial exception to the opinions of his wife, provided he added the word "darling" — and meant it.

In differing with others, a friendly attitude can be far more effective than antagonism or grumpiness. In short, disagree without getting disagreeable.

It is easy to be abrupt, blunt, and even sarcastic when things don't go our way. But little taunts and stinging sneers carelessly flung, especially at the young, tend to stifle and embitter.

Firmness and discipline are most effective when blended with love.

Each of us has been endowed by God with the ability to be a distributor of His divine love. Develop this capacity within you.

Be the first to smooth troubled waters in your home, at work, on the bus, at school, in fact everywhere, and you will find yourself wanting to reach out to wider horizons.

Yes, put love where there is no love and you will find love!

All will know that you are My disciples, if you have love for one another. (Jn. 13:35)

Deepen in me, Savior, a yearning to be Your instrument for bringing Your love to my world.

Heroic Policeman Saves 12

A Chicago policeman played the role of hero by shielding 12 children from a runaway car.

The officer, Thomas Tobin, 56, was directing traffic at a busy intersection when he suddenly saw a fast-moving auto heading for the youngsters.

Hurling himself into the midst of the 12 children as they crossed the street, the policeman succeeded in knocking all of them out of the way of the careening car. He did not fare so well, however, and was struck and dragged 20 feet by the speeding auto.

Although few public servants need risk their lives in such a manner, their day-to-day dedication to duty proves they sincerely desire to honor God by working for the best interests of their fellow man.

We hear much about the few in public office who violate their trust but too little about those who are conscientiously striving to live up to their responsibilities.

Focus attention on those who are doing an honest, upright job and you will do much to strengthen your government.

Blessed are those servants whom the Master finds awake when He comes . . . He will gird Himself and have them sit at table, and He will come and serve them. (Lk. 12:37)

Bless all those, Divine Master, who devote themselves to government administration.

Watch That Honk

Most auto horn-honking is nothing more than a display of bad manners. That is the conclusion Philadelphia officials reached after an extensive study at six of the city's busiest intersections.

"Ninety percent of the horn honks are attributable to impatience," was one investigator's summary of the survey.

Whether driving a car, riding in a bus, shopping in a supermarket, or partaking in the activities of the family circle, there are countless precious opportunities to show that you truly love others, not merely put up with them.

Make the most of each occasion to practice the Christ-like principle of treating others as you would like to have them treat you. It is a divine art that pays rich dividends the more it is practiced.

Putting up with the defects of others, even those who tempt you to honk your horn too much, will stimulate you to reach out to wider horizons with the love and truth of Christ.

If anyone forces you to go one mile, go with him two miles. (Mt. 5:41)

Call on me, Lord, to be a distributor of Your all-embracing love.

One Tiny Match

Some years ago I learned an important lesson at the Metropolitan Opera House in New York. There was no performance — in fact, the house was empty. The manager, who was showing me the theater, asked me to wait in the back while he put on the house lights.

I could scarcely see him as he went down the aisle. When he got up on stage, he lit a match to see where he was going.

From the last row in the orchestra I could clearly see that tiny match. Insignificant as this pinpoint of light was, it was still greater than all the darkness. All that was needed to remove the darkness completely was to multiply that flame a million times.

In a matter of moments the manager did just that. He turned on the switches and the great opera house was flooded with light.

Even the least individual can be a transmitter of the light of Christ by applying His divine truth and love to every facet of life. Remember, "it is better to light one candle than to curse the darkness."

Jesus spoke to them, saying, "I am the light of the world." (Jn. 8:12)

Teach me to light candles, loving Jesus, not blow them out.

100,000 Matches

Over 100,000 spectators jammed the Los Angeles Coliseum one evening, just after World War II, to witness a pageant in honor of the city's war heroes.

The huge audience was reminded that each of them, despite any feeling of insignificance, should play an important role in restoring peace to the world.

To dramatize the power of one individual, all the lights in the great arena were suddenly turned off. Then the master of ceremonies struck a match and held it aloft. The tiny flame, visible to everyone, clearly showed the far-reaching effect of one little light.

The speaker then urged each one present to light his own match. In a matter of moments nearly 100,000 pinpoints of light lit up the summer sky. Quickly and effectively each saw the importance of his own participation.

Bring the light of Christ into the darkness and you will accomplish much good.

Let your light so shine before men, that they may see your good works and give glory to your Father who is in heaven. (Mt. 5:16)

Grant, O Lord, that I may learn that it is indeed "better to light one candle than to curse the darkness."

More Than Oil Needed

You would probably be delighted if you hit oil in your back yard.

But when that happened to one man in Tulsa, Ok., he actually protested: "But I don't want an oil well, all I want is a water well." His wife objected to the strike, saying: "I can't wash my dishes in oil."

The problem was soon solved. Although oil oozed out on all sides, workers kept drilling and eventually found water. So he ended up with both water and oil.

It is important to keep first things first during our pilgrimage through life. It is not always easy to distinguish between essentials and non-essentials. But those who conscientiously try usually bring a special blessing on their lives.

Anyone who ignores the true and enduring goals set for him by God and concentrates on the pursuit of such incidentals as wealth, power, and pleasure sooner or later loses out in every way.

Seek (your Father's) kingdom and these things will be yours. (Lk. 12:31)

Help me, Jesus, to be single-hearted in seeking You in all things.

Be the Master Always

A speeding, out-of-control auto brought death to its 49-year-old driver in Cincinnati.

A police officer, seeing the fast-moving car, gave chase. When he drew alongside of it, he shouted to the lady behind the wheel to "pull over to the curb."

"I can't stop the car," she cried out.

"Turn off the ignition key," he directed.

"I can't find it," she shouted back.

Within seconds the car careened down a hill. The bewildered driver couldn't cope with the curve at the bottom. She crashed into a pole and was killed.

It is a fearful thing when a human being loses mastery of anything over which he or she should have control.

Whether it's a speeding car or the less tangible but deadly passions of pride, greed, or lust, we flirt with catastrophe if we allow ourselves to be dominated by those things over which God expects us to be the master under all circumstances.

Everyone who commits sin is a slave to sin. (Jn. 8:34)

Help me, Lord, to overcome my weaknesses, not become the slave of them.

Behind the Daring of Columbus

On Aug. 3, 1492, Christopher Columbus and his fleet of three tiny ships lifted anchor in Palos, Portugal, and started westward on a long and dangerous voyage.

Conditions aboard the little vessels were far from ideal. The usual diet was salt meat, which often became rancid, and dried peas with a little wine and water.

Time and time again the frightened sailors tried to persuade Columbus to return. They were on the verge of mutiny just before the first glimpse of the New World was finally sighted on the morning of Oct. 12.

Behind the big vision and daring faith that carried Christopher Columbus through every heartbreaking obstacle was the conviction that he was a Christ-bearer serving God's purpose and the well-being of all.

If you wish to leave the world better than you found it, you, too, must pay the price of suffering. But for all eternity you will rejoice in the fact that you, too, were a Christ-bearer.

Many are the afflictions of the righteous; but the Lord delivers them out of them all. (Ps. 34:19)

Spirit of Wisdom, enable me to brave all difficulties to achieve the potential You have given me.

Make the Most of Life

A hard-working father lost his life one day while building a 15 x 30 foot swimming pool for his wife and three children.

The 39-year-old man worked as a mailman by day and as a supermarket clerk by night. Every minute of spare time went into the pool.

He had nearly finished the job. All that remained was to drain out some rain water. He borrowed an electric pump for this final task.

When nearly all the water had been removed, the happy man hopped into the empty pool barefooted to lift out the pump. Suddenly he screamed and collapsed while his family looked on. He had accidentally stepped on an exposed electric wire and was immediately electrocuted.

None of us has a lease on life. We can be summoned quite suddenly to the judgment seat to render an account of our stewardship.

Whether your years on earth be many or few, make the most of them as a preparation for eternity.

Watch therefore, for you know neither the day nor the hour. (Mt. 25:13)

Jesus, Savior, show me how to build now for eternity.

Never Trust a Friendly Rattler

Man's best friend is definitely not a rattlesnake, a 22-year-old pet lover found out to his dismay.

The young laborer came across a reptile in the desert near Denver and found it such a friendly creature that he decided to take it home with him.

For several days the serpent's behavior was above reproach. On the third day, however, he posed with the snake for a photographer. Then, unexpectedly, without the slightest warning, it sank its fangs into the young man's hand.

Crushed with disappointment, he told his visitors: "I can't understand it; we've been the best of friends."

Much of the world's tragedy can be traced to the confidence that well-meaning persons have placed in those whose evil intent they should have recognized.

Stick to God's truth and your own common sense and you will not endanger your welfare or that of others.

Beware of false prophets, who come to you in sheep's clothing but inwardly are ravenous wolves. (Mt. 7:15)

Guide me, Wisdom of the Father, so that I may not be deceived by those whose bad intentions are only too evident.

A Teenage Samaritan

An Iowa man who had been hearing a lot about juvenile delinquency went to his office one night to catch up on some work.

He returned to his car hours later only to find a note lying on the front seat.

"You left your lights on," it read, "so if your battery is dead, that's why. I turned the lights off at 9:40. You're welcome."

It was signed by a student in a local high school. And the car's engine did start.

There are those who loudly complain about the misdeeds of young people, but who never think to give them credit for the good that so many do.

The only way to make juvenile delinquency a thing of the past is to stimulate more and more young people to set a worthy goal in life and pursue it.

God will bless you if you praise the solid accomplishments of teenagers and help them to accomplish even more.

Let us not grow weary in well-doing, for in due season we shall reap, if we do not lose heart. (Gal. 6:9)

Father, show me how to build up not tear down.

He Left More Than Money

When Gene Fowler, newspaper writer and author, died, he left an unusual will. In it he expressed the hope that his wife, to whom he left more than $10,000, would approve "the fact that I have given such small attention to the material prizes of the world."

The nobility of the career which Fowler regarded as a holy vocation was reflected in this explanatory comment:

"There comes a time in the life of every artist when he must decide between the objectives of moneyed ease and/or the sure prospect of lonely struggle and sacrifice and lack of recognition until he grows old or is dead. The latter choice was mine."

If your life is marked by an unselfish determination to inspire or better the lives of others, you'll probably never get rich or leave a fortune. But you'll certainly leave the world better than you found it and make an investment that will last for all eternity.

> **Charge (the rich) not to be haughty, nor to set their hopes on uncertain riches but on God who richly furnishes us with everything to enjoy. They are to do good. (1 Tim. 6:17-18)**

May I put into life, not merely take out, Son of God.

'Dead Man' Still Lives

A man who was pronounced dead by doctors said he was "feeling fine" two years later.

When the 76-year-old patient stopped breathing and his heart appeared to give out, two doctors gave up hope for him.

A half hour later they were happily surprised by a nurse's aide who told them that she had just seen the "dead" man's eyes flutter and his arms move.

The amazed doctors rushed back and resumed the treatment they had been giving the elderly man. This time it was successful.

Medical science has made remarkable strides in prolonging human life — and even in keeping the spark of life aglow against all odds.

But at best such gains are temporary. The years that God has loaned us are comparatively few. The important thing is to use them in an untiring search for ways to leave the world a better place than we found it. Then they will count as a meaningful preparation for eternity.

A thousand years in Your sight are but as yesterday when it is past, or a watch in the night. (Ps. 90:4)

Give us a share of Your wisdom, Holy Spirit, that we may have a "heart of wisdom."

Hungry Cats Find a Friend

Alley cats in Auckland, New Zealand, can usually count on at least one good meal a day, thanks to the solicitude of one thoughtful woman.

Each evening she loads up her car with large quantities of liver, milk, scraps of meat and other cat food given her by well-wishers and local hotels.

Making up to 15 stops a night in the dimly lit back streets of the city, she feeds an average of 60 of the animals.

When people show reasonable care for all God's creatures they enhance their own human dignity. How much more, then, does it redound to their credit when they show an outgoing concern for the living conditions of their fellow humans.

Millions upon millions of people over the world go to sleep every night gnawed by the pangs of hunger. Many more, probably two-thirds of humanity, suffer from malnutrition. Christ will bless you abundantly if you strive to relieve their distress.

Hungry and thirsty, their soul fainted within them. (Ps. 107:5)

Never let me shut my heart, O merciful God, to those who need my help.

Insurance That Counts

"Nothing ever happens around here, I don't need accident insurance." That was the brush-off given an insurance sales agent by a mechanic working on an automobile.

The words were hardly out of the mechanic's mouth when a spark from a wrench ignited an open can of gasoline. In a few moments the whole repair shop was ablaze.

Fortunately the garage worker was uninjured. But as soon as the fire was under control, the worker asked the insurance agent to write up a policy then and there.

It is never wise to be careless about our material affairs, but in the case of our eternal salvation, too much is at stake to take foolish risks.

Be sure to insure yourself against all hazards by filling each day with good works which honor God and benefit your fellow human beings. If you do, you will be taking out a divine policy that costs little but is a safeguard for time and eternity.

Beware of all covetousness; for a man's life does not consist in the abundance of his possessions. (Lk. 12:15)

Guide me, Lord, to take all steps necessary to make my life worthwhile in Your sight.

He Took the Hard Way

Climbing down a chimney is not the easiest way to enter one's home. Harry McVeigh, 44, of Altmore, Northern Ireland, found that out the hard way.

He was locked out of his new house with nobody inside to let him in. He could not persuade himself to break a window or force a door.

So he climbed up on the roof and started down the chimney. He had descended only a few feet when he found himself lodged in a tight squeeze, unable to go up or down.

Thirteen hours later, and after many cries in vain for help, a passerby came to his rescue. After being hauled out of the chimney at the end of a rope, he wasted no time in forcing a door to get into his new home.

All of us can slip into difficulties. But to avoid making a bad situation still worse, we would do well to stick to the sound, reasonable principles that God wishes us to live by. We can save ourselves many a jam if we do.

Great peace have those who love Your law; nothing can make them stumble. (Ps. 119:165)

Thanks to You, Father, for giving us a plan of life that leads to life eternal with You.

Prodding Brings Corrective Action

One man renovated a union because his sister took it upon herself to prod him gently but persistently about his moral obligation to attend meetings and make his voice heard. He had deliberately stayed away because his local was dominated by a radical minority.

She kept emphasizing these two points:

■ He had no right to complain about conditions if he didn't bother to attend meetings.

■ One big reason why corrupt or subversive forces gain control is precisely that honest, competent people are not on the job.

Eventually the reluctant man began to attend meetings. He soon saw what one person could accomplish despite all obstacles. He persuaded other members to take part in union activities. As a result of their combined positive action, new life was injected into the union.

You, too, can right many a wrong in the world, with God's help, if you come to grips with problems, not evade them.

> **He does not withdraw His eyes from the righteous, but with kings upon the throne he sets them for ever, and they are exalted. (Job 36:7)**

> *Deepen in me, Lord, such a reverence for truth that I will always be its champion.*

Finds Teaching Vocation in Mid-Life

"If you're not interested in others, you're in trouble," was the considered opinion of a 38-year-old Tennessee man.

Although he had been earning a good salary and had a liberal expense account and four weeks vacation with pay, he was not satisfied.

"I wanted to make a contribution," he confided to a friend. "To me, that seemed to be the only real satisfaction a man can find."

He decided to be a teacher and took night courses to prepare for his new vocation.

"For me," he said, "teaching is my way of contributing to a better society — maybe not to mine, but at least to a better society for my children."

Now that he is giving education courses in a Southern university, he no longer earns the same salary but finds his inner satisfaction worth the financial loss.

You may not be in a position to enter the teaching field yourself, but you can serve God and your fellow human beings well by encouraging others to do so.

Who does (the commandments) and teaches them shall be called great in the kingdom of heaven. (Mt. 5:19)

Remind me, Divine Teacher, always to have a high regard for learning which benefits Your children.

People Need Music

"Music produces a kind of pleasure which human nature cannot do without," was the tribute paid by the Chinese sage, Confucius, 500 years before Christ.

All through history the human spirit has been elevated by the beauty of inspiring music.

In fact, Shakespeare went so far as to say:

"The man that hath no music in himself,
Nor is not moved with concord of sweet sounds,
Is fit for treasons, stratagems, and spoils . . .
Let no such man be trusted."

In these times when so much emphasis is put on the physical and material aspects of life, there is danger of overlooking the cultural, intellectual and spiritual. Human beings hunger for the nourishing effects of that beauty which is a reflection of God's beauty.

Encourage music that elevates rather than debases and you will be making a contribution to the common good.

There is no better place to begin than with young persons, who can carry this good taste through life.

Out of heaven He let you hear His voice, that He might discipline you. (Dt. 4:36)

Thanks, loving Creator, for the manifestation of Your truth, goodness and beauty in music.

A Systematic Burglar

A London burglar, who had broken into about 120 homes, calmly told police that he pursues his strange avocation on a four-hour-a-day basis, exclusive of weekends.

He explained to the officers that all of his burglarizing was done "between 10 a.m. and 2 p.m. from Monday to Friday, as I never go out stealing on Saturday or Sunday."

One who is so orderly and systematic about thievery could probably become a great saint if he ever channeled his ability in the right direction.

No matter how far we drift away from the divine plan into error, evil, or ugliness, we are capable of living nobly and constructively.

In takes much faith, hope, and charity to persevere in the difficult task of redeeming or rehabilitating those who fall by the wayside.

But one always makes some gains and has the constant joy of knowing that one is doing the work of the Redeemer.

I came not to call the righteous, but sinners. (Mt. 9:13)

Have mercy, Crucified Lord, on we who slip and fall.
Help us to put our good qualities to worthwhile use.

Keep a Sense of Proportion

An over-dressed vagrant surprised police when they arrested him in Memphis.

The 25-year-old man looked like a turtle, his head barely showing above a heavy brown coat. Police discovered that he was actually wearing 11 coats, including a leather jacket and an army coat, 16 pairs of trousers, 3 shirts and red flannels.

He told police that he liked to be warm when traveling. Then too, he added, his duffle bag would not hold anything more.

When a passion for accumulating things dominates the life of any one of us, we can gradually lose a sense of proportion. We become the victim of a craving that nothing can satisfy.

Under all circumstances remain master of yourself and you will enjoy that peace of mind, heart and soul that God promises to all who put to good use the countless blessings of creation.

In short, make sure that you never become possessed by your possessions.

Beware of all covetousness; for a man's life does not consist in the abundance of his possessions. (Lk. 12:15)

Help me, O Lord, to avoid covetousness in all its many forms.

The Qualities of a Good Teacher

"What nobler employment, or more valuable to the state, than that of a man who instructs the rising generation?" asks Cicero.

In our own day, Mrs. Susan M. Dorsey wrote the following tribute to the teacher:

"When we speak of the inspiration of the schools, we think at once of the teacher whose personality: 1) inspires respect and confidence; 2) provokes effort; 3) makes indolence and indifference seem unworthy; 4) arouses ambition, and 5) whose knowledge and wisdom are a constant lure to effort on the part of students."

Teachers who see in each of their students someone made in God's image will always surmount difficulties that their vital profession entails.

Work in every possible way to guarantee for teachers the respect and assistance they deserve. After all, they are your partners and the benefactors of everyone.

> **Those who are wise shall shine like the brightness of the firmament; and those who turn many to righteousness, like the stars for ever and ever. (Dan. 12:3)**

Divine Teacher, instill in me a reverence for learning.

Safety Talk Spoiled

Five minutes after a broadcast on the virtues of safe driving a radio commentator became involved in an accident of his own.

After colliding with another car, and causing extensive damage to each vehicle, the disappointed broadcaster said: "Now I'm just a 'has been' safe driver."

To increase his embarrassment, the eloquent advocate of safe driving had become eligible that day for a reduction in his auto insurance coverage.

Achieving a noble goal is one thing, but maintaining it requires vigilance and effort.

The easiest way to crush your laurels is to sit on them. Complacency or self-satisfaction can be fatal. In pursuing truth and justice, take nothing for granted. Remember that as long as you are in this life, you can become the victim of your own human weaknesses.

Only when you have finished the course and are safe in heaven, will you be able to relax.

For freedom Christ has set us free; stand fast therefore, and do not submit again to a yoke of slavery. (Gal. 5:1)

Lord, strengthen me to practice what I preach.

The Penalty of Cowardice

"To know what is right and not to do it is the worst cowardice," said Confucius in 500 B.C.

Shakespeare sounded the same note when he said: "Cowards die many times before their deaths; the valiant never taste of death but once."

According to the very nature that God gives us, every person is made to uphold what is good and true. We hurt ourselves and even do violence to our nature if we withhold the personal contribution that we should be making to a just and orderly world.

Try as we may, we cannot quiet our conscience when it tells us we should face instead of evade problems whether they shape our own destiny or that of our family, friends or humankind in general.

You can be spared the tortures of cowardice if you resolve before the Lord to live up to what He expects of you.

Far better, you will experience the peace and joy of heart, mind and soul that is the reward of those who truly love God above all else and others as themselves.

Perfect love casts out fear. For fear has to do with punishment, and he who fears is not perfected in love. We love, because He first loved us. (1 Jn. 4:18-19)

Give me the love, Jesus, to face my responsibilities rather than evade them.

Teenager Proves Hero

A teenager braved flames in a Philadelphia apartment house three times to save two young cousins and his dog.

When the 16-year-old boy awoke and found the ceiling of his third-floor room ablaze he grabbed the baby and fought his way through smoke down to the second floor.

After handing the child to a policeman, he dashed back upstairs and carried his brother to the street.

Then for the third time he went back to the burning room to rescue his dog, trapped under a burning bed.

In times of emergency young people often display an alertness, initiative and enterprise that they themselves do not realize they possess.

There will be great hope for the world when adults become more keenly aware of the reservoir of goodness that God has instilled in every boy and girl. Do your part to put it to good use.

Be strong and very courageous. (Jos. 1:7)

Enable young people, O Lord, to put to good use the powers You have entrusted to them.

Watch Where You Are Going

Digging a 515-foot tunnel with a teaspoon would be a grueling ordeal under any circumstances. But it was almost too much for one convict under life sentence.

After spending 16 months in digging what he thought was a sure way to freedom, his tunnel ended in another prisoner's cell in the disciplinary block, the most carefully guarded part of the jail.

He did not discover his mistake until the last few spoonfuls. Then it became clear that, despite all his careful planning and dogged persistence, he had miscalculated one of the most important details of all — where he was going.

Some people go through life pursuing goals that lead nowhere or, worse still, to the very troubles they seek to avoid.

If you base all you think, say, and do on the changeless truths of Christ, you will know in your heart that you are headed in a direction that leads to happiness both here and hereafter.

The Lord has made everything for its purpose. (Prov. 16:4)

Keep me close to Your truth, Holy Spirit, so that I will not stray into trouble.

She Didn't Forget

When a welfare department receives a $4,000 check from someone who has been on relief it is a heartening surprise for everyone.

On the back of the check was written the words: "To the New York City Department of Welfare, in payment for money given in desperate times."

Officials said this was one of the largest voluntary reimbursements ever received by the department.

An investigation disclosed that 25 years earlier the donor was forced to go on relief when her husband abandoned her and her children.

As her family grew older, the mother took a part-time job and eventually went off the relief rolls. Later she came into a small inheritance.

Once the wolf was away from her own door, she returned the money so that it could be used for the needs of others.

Show your gratitude for the blessings of God by seeking practical ways to bring solace to those worse off than you are.

A brother helped is like a strong city. (Prov. 18:19)

Teach me to think of others less fortunate than I, Master, not just of my own needs, wants and desires.

Truth in Advertising

Honesty got quick results for a 15-year-old Rhode Island boy one summer.

In a newspaper advertisement, he frankly stated that he wanted to sell a "Leaky boat, a worn outboard motor, rusty tongs — all for $50."

"I was swamped with calls and I sold the gear," the boy triumphantly told his friends.

There is something refreshing about a person who is open and sincere, not simply because honesty pays but because he is convinced he should be true to God, to himself and everybody else.

You can do your part to restore honesty to the marketplace by sticking to the facts rather than resorting to evasions or glossing over knowledge to which others have a right.

Keep in mind that an honest world starts with you as much as with anybody. If you live continually in the presence of God, you will better comprehend the deep meaning of the old proverb: "Of all crafts, to be an honest man is the master craft."

Let us conduct ourselves becomingly. (Rom. 13:13)

Give me, Holy Spirit, the wisdom and fortitude to do the "hard right" rather than the "easy wrong."

Even Machines Can Err

The capacity to make mistakes is not reserved exclusively to humans.

When an employee in Jacksonville, N.C., did not receive his regular wages one week, the company wired California asking the concern that took care of such matters what had happened.

The reply came with this terse comment: "Our infallible electronic computer goofed."

Most of us make our share of errors in the course of a lifetime, so we can derive a bit of wry amusement from a machine that does the same.

But our great advantage is that, as human beings, we can profit by our mistakes.

Rather than be disheartened by occasional mistakes, learn from them to do better next time in your efforts to serve God and your fellow human beings.

Beloved . . . beware lest you be carried away with the error of lawless men and lose your own stability. (2 Pet. 3:17)

Help me, God of mercies, to respond to my failures with a determination to grow wiser because of them.

One Way to Improve Arithmetic

A classroom grocery store has been giving added practical meaning to arithmetic for fourth-grade students in a Hamilton, Ont., public school.

The resourceful teacher, anxious to relate figures to everyday living, decided to set up the miniature store in a corner of the classroom.

He showed his pupils how to stock and price merchandise and then divided them into businessmen, consumers, storekeepers and clerks. Play money was used for purchases.

The youngsters found the practical usage of addition, subtraction and multiplication so intriguing that their arithmetic marks went up 20 percent and not one pupil failed the course.

You will find a similar realistic challenge if you seek ways and means to apply divine principles to the little and big problems of modern life.

Better still, you will realize you can be a co-laborer with God in bringing the order of heaven down to earth.

Your kingdom come, Your will be done, on earth as it is in heaven. (Mt. 6:10)

Jesus, show me how to do the will of our Father in heaven.

Final Look

A desperate hunt for a four-year-old girl in New Brunswick, N.J., turned out happily when a searcher took "one last look."

For hours 150 volunteers had scoured the snow-covered lanes without success, and finally abandoned their efforts.

One man, however, decided around midnight to go back to the girl's home for one last attempt.

Passing a narrow alley he spotted a pile of untrampled snow and heard what "sounded like a puppy moaning." Digging with his hands he broke through to the little one, who had been missing for about 10 hours.

Although perseverance is not always crowned with success, there is no success without it. Whether it is in a search for a lost child or for reasonable economies in government, the Lord blesses those who refuse to take "no" for an answer.

The welfare of others may depend on your ability to set a high goal and stick to it.

No one who puts his hand to the plow and looks back is fit for the kingdom of God. (Lk. 9:62)

Father, bless me with perseverance in carrying out Your will.

Singer With a Mission

"Singers have a glorious mission, to transmit to their audience all the musical beauties that lie in opera."

So said Giovanni Martinelli, a world-famed tenor who sang with New York's Metropolitan Opera for 30 years.

The person imbued with the conviction that he or she has been entrusted by God with a mission to fulfill in life usually experiences the true joy of living.

On the other hand, the one who has little or no concept of the special role he or she is expected to play on the stage of life ordinarily leads a dull, aimless, purposeless existence.

In God's plan, you too have been given a personal assignment to transmit to all a bit of divine truth, goodness, and beauty. It should be a glorious mission for you because you can make the world better for your being in it.

As the Father has sent Me, even so I send you. (Jn. 20:21)

Awaken in me, God, a keen realization of the mission in life which You have given me to fulfill and give me the strength to live it.

How to Personalize an Election

A part-time bartender once won a Nebraska election without giving any speeches or having any campaign cards or posters printed.

This enterprising individual had no phone, so he conducted his campaign from his sister's home.

He used a unique person-to-person formula and made it a point to talk each day with as many people as possible. Those whom he could not meet personally, he reached by telephone.

Slowly but surely this unflagging campaigner contacted hundreds and then thousands of individuals. People gradually became disposed to him because he took the time and trouble to contact them personally, instead of relying on the impersonal billboards and posters.

Those who strive to restore spiritual values to the marketplace should make an even greater effort to personalize all they do.

The warm, living, spoken word is always more powerful than anything written, forceful as it may be.

By your words you will be justified, and by your words you will be condemned. (Mt. 12:37)

Help me to personalize all I do for You and others, Lord.

Wisdom Cannot Be Bought

A 26-year-old graduate of an Eastern university brought suit against the institution. He claimed that the college detained him falsely by professing to teach wisdom.

A superior court judge dismissed the young man's plea on the grounds that "wisdom cannot be taught."

No one receives wisdom on a silver spoon. It is acquired only through personal inconvenience and hardship. An old Welsh proverb puts it very well: "All wisdom must be paid for with pain."

All that the home, church, or school can do is to present the principles of true wisdom. It is up to each individual to apply them to his or her own life and the world in which he or she lives. Such an individual will grow in wisdom even when they give it away.

Be more than humanly wise. By meditation, prayer, and effort cultivate divine wisdom and thus add meaning and purpose to daily living.

Keep ever aware that this life is nothing more than a stepping-stone to the everlasting happiness of the next.

If any of you lacks wisdom, let him ask God, who gives to all ... and it will be given. (Jas. 1:5)

Deepen in me, Holy Spirit, a reverence for divine wisdom.

The Devil's Way

A friend who has had considerable difficulty keeping a very worthy organization alive claims that most of the trouble comes from within, not from without. It is well summarized in the following list of ways to demolish any organization:

- Don't come to the meetings.
- If you do come, come late.
- If you attend a meeting, find fault with the work of the officers and other members.
- Never accept an office, as it is easier to criticize than to do things.
- Feel hurt if you are not appointed to a committee, but if you are, do not attend committee meetings.
- If asked by the chair to give your opinion on some matter, reply that you have nothing to say. After the meeting, tell everyone how things ought to have been done.
- Do nothing more than is absolutely necessary, but when other members roll up their sleeves and work unselfishly, say that the board is run by a clique.
- Hold back your dues as long as possible, or don't pay them at all.
- Don't bother about getting new members. Let someone else do it.

Drive out a scoffer, and strife will go out, and quarreling and abuse will cease. (Prov. 22:10)

Pray that I may be honest in my judgment of myself and generous in my judgment of others, Lord.

Lighting Candles: Indian Style

A man in India is doing his part to change the world. He switched his job as a supervisor in an industrial plant to the more influential one of instructor.

Here is an excerpt from a letter sent to The Christophers.

"Though my job is purely technical, I still get enough opportunities to impress upon the students the importance of loving one's own job and of seeing the harmony and order in every bit of mechanism as arranged by God through nature, and thus, the necessity for thanking God at every step for creating such physical laws."

"In a hundred and one ways," he concluded, "it is possible to light a candle instead of cursing the darkness."

There is nothing earth-shaking about this case. But perhaps this young man, multiplied millions of times over, can make God's "peace on earth" an attainable goal.

No matter what your position, world peace begins with you.

Those among the people who are wise shall make many understand. (Dan. 11:33)

Help me know, Holy Spirit, that my small efforts are unique and invaluable.

How to Combat Vandalism

School property is seldom damaged when students appreciate that the institution is theirs just as much as it is anybody's.

Such was the conclusion of Nathan Goldman of Syracuse University after a two-year study.

He found that "When members of the school group have a sense of belonging to the school, and when they feel that the school belongs to them, morale tends to be high and damage low."

When, however, there is a "couldn't care less" attitude on the part of the young people, the resulting boredom often leads to vandalism.

The energies of youthful troublemakers can be turned from liabilities into assets once they come to realize that they are entrusted by God with talents that can help everybody.

Do all in your power to remind students that they are both needed and wanted in improving the little world of their schools and the bigger world into which they will soon go.

Have we not all one Father? Has not one God created us? Why then are we faithless to one another, profaning the covenant? (Mal. 2:10)

Promote in us, Father, a spirit of mutual cooperation and respect.

No Man Is an Island

It's hard for any of us to realize that anytime another suffers, we also are affected. But if we are true to our Christian belief, this is exactly the case.

As John Donne, the famous English poet, wrote several hundred years ago:

"All mankind is of one Author . . . No man is an island, entire of itself. Every man is a piece of the continent, a part of the main. If a clod be washed away by the sea, Europe is the less . . . Any man's death diminishes me, because I am involved in mankind."

Many people today have a "leave-me-alone" point of view; they don't want to "get involved" in anything. But the fact of the matter is that they are, as Donne says, "involved in mankind." When they realize this and act in harmony with their fellow human beings, they begin to live more fully.

We, though many, are one body in Christ, and individually members one of another. (Rom. 12:5)

Enable me, Creator, to incorporate in my life the reality that I am brother or sister to all.

The More We Give

While in Milan some time ago I tried to find someone who spoke English. Finally, a young couple was pointed out to me, with the suggestion that perhaps they might be able to help me.

"I speak English, though not much," the woman volunteered in answer to my question. "But I'm teaching it to Carlo here" — she indicated her companion. "I find the best way to learn English myself is to teach it to someone else."

It was worth the trip to Milan just to hear this one remark which expresses so well an important Christopher idea: the more we give the more we get.

In the truest sense, one of the best ways to keep one's faith is to "give it away." On the other hand, one of the easiest ways to lose one's faith is to "keep it to one's self."

I have no silver and gold, but I give you what I have. (Acts 3:6)

Pray that even those who have some little glimmer of the truth may share it with those who have none.

Expect Difficulties

When Benjamin Disraeli was asked why he persevered in the face of great obstacles, he gave a bit of advice that should interest all who are tempted to give up when working for a good cause.

"Have you ever watched a stonecutter at work?" he asked. "He will hammer away at a rock for perhaps a hundred times without a crack showing in it. Then, at the one hundred and first blow, it will split in two.

"It is not alone that blow that accomplishes the result, but the hundred others that went before, as well."

It is often difficult for many to keep working away when they see no results. Usually they are counting on too easy a victory.

On the other hand, if they expected a worthwhile job to require a hundred efforts, they would be less likely to falter when they have gone only two thirds of the way.

Working for the glory of God and the good of all is not easy.

> **Do not think that I have come to bring peace on earth; I have not come to bring peace, but a sword. (Mt. 10:34)**

> *Jesus, enable me to accept the sacrifices that You promised would be the lot of a Christ-bearer.*

Telling the World

Most of us have frequent occasion to be grateful to God for special blessings He has showered upon us. But how few show our gratitude by telling others of His goodness; urging them to take heart.

One small boy in Providence, R.I., however, did "tell the world." He sent this message to the local paper which gave it prominent display:

"Dear Sir:

"I prayed to God to make my mother get better and I want to thank God so when He reads the paper He can see it.

"From a little boy who loves God. May God thank you."

What mattered to the child was that God should be publicly thanked. In this way he sent a heartening proof of God's care to thousands who may not have been aware of it or who may have forgotten it.

Let your light so shine before men, that they may see your good works and give glory to your Father who is in heaven. (Mt. 5:16)

Help me, Lord, to show my gratitude to You by sharing with others the blessings You have showered upon me.

Ancient Tree Felled in an Hour

In the space of an hour the growth of 20 centuries crashed to the ground. A giant California redwood tree, estimated to be 2,000 years old, was cut down for its lumber. There was enough to build 20 five-room bungalows.

This redwood was probably a mere sapling when Christ was born.

When St. Paul was thrown in prison in A.D. 58, it was more than 60 feet high.

When Rome fell, it was about 150 feet tall and 10 feet thick near its base.

When the Magna Charta was signed in 1215, this giant of the forest stretched up 250 feet.

As this redwood tree was cut down, so many of the great gains made through the centuries by Judeo-Christian civilization are being eliminated today. Many advances such as God's gifts of religion, peace, freedom and culture are disappearing from the lives of millions.

A change for the better will come only when enough like you make it your business to restore Judeo-Christian principles to the marketplace.

Think not that I have come to abolish the law and the prophets; I have come not to abolish them but to fulfill them. (Mt. 5:17)

Lord, help me to do my share in bringing back to all phases of life the truths that make us free.

Much More Than a Backache

A man who complained of a backache found to his astonishment that he had a broken neck.

The 50-year-old man walked into a California hospital several hours after an automobile accident and asked a doctor to help him find out what was wrong with his back.

The doctor, fearful that there might be some internal injury that he couldn't detect, ordered an X-ray. It revealed that the man had broken his neck.

Hospital officials said that the victim had come in the nick of time. If he had jarred or twisted his neck sharply, he would have died or been paralyzed.

Don't neglect either bodily pain or the pangs of conscience. They are warning signs of more trouble than meets the eye.

Rather than diagnose your physical or spiritual ills in a superficial way and run the risk of making a bad situation more serious, seek the advice of experts in getting to the heart of the trouble.

Apply your mind to instruction and your ear to words of knowledge. (Pr. 23:12)

Grant me Your courage, Holy Spirit, to seek the whole truth regardless of the cost.

Set Big Goals for Yourself

"Make no little plans. They have no magic to stir one's blood. Make big plans, aim high in hope and work." That's the advice one expert gives to those who dream of success.

You will never bring out the bit of greatness within you if you set your sights low.

No matter how insignificant your role in life may seem, it is important. You have been delegated by God Almighty to help a world which too few are bothering to try to save.

You are endowed with a capacity to embrace the whole world and everybody in it with your love. The more you develop your own great potential by setting big goals for yourself, the more meaning and purpose you will add to your life while benefiting countless others.

Christ told the fishermen He chose as His apostles to overcome their inclination to smallness. He bade them tackle the task of fishing in a daring way.

Put out into the deep and let down your nets for a catch. (Lk. 5:4)

Let all that I think, say and do, Jesus, be motivated by divine generosity, not human smallness.

Know How to Give Advice

"Advice is not disliked because it is advice, but because so few people know how to give it." This wise observation was made by the English writer, Leigh Hunt, in 1821.

The following tips may help you to be more effective in expressing your viewpoint:

■ Submit suggestions, don't try to impose them on those who merely invite your opinion.

■ Use such expressions as "I think" or "it seems to me" rather than give the impression your view should be taken as the "final word."

■ If your advice is not accepted, take it gracefully. By being impatient, you indicate you care more about having your own way than you do about the judgment of the person who honored you by asking your advice.

■ When you are convinced that your view is for the greater good, take gentle, persevering steps to win better understanding for it. Don't jeopardize a good opinion by becoming too domineering.

In short, just show simple Christian consideration for others in all that you think, say, and do.

As you wish that men would do to you, do so to them. (Lk. 6:31)

Teach me, Spirit of God, to learn how to disagree without being disagreeable.

Rough Ride for a Cat

Little dreaming that the family cat was nestled in the half-dry wash, a housewife in Florida bundled the sheets into a clothes dryer.

When a strange bumping developed, she called her husband to investigate. He opened the door of the dryer and the haggard pet staggered out, more dead than alive.

Its tongue was parched and hanging out, its hair stood on end, and it had no more than a glassy stare for the family.

The startled husband tried to help the cat, but the terrified animal nipped his hand. Happily, both cat and husband recovered.

Many times we fail to get recognition or thanks for our efforts. Don't be too surprised if those who have suffered seem ungrateful when you go out of your way to help them.

Make allowance for them in Christ's name. The important thing is that you have done your part.

Do good . . . expecting nothing in return; and your reward will be great. (Lk. 6:35)

Help me, O my Savior, to show an understanding heart toward those who seem ungrateful.

Children Catch Thief

A teenage thief, who had stolen a $10 roll of quarters from a service station operator's car, wondered how anyone saw him bury his loot under a tree.

But when he was taken to police headquarters, he was confronted by two children who had witnessed his operation from their perch in the branches of the same tree.

The young thief had been running an errand in the station owner's car. The children were quiet but alert witnesses. After seeing him stop en route and hide the money, they immediately notified the police.

Deeds, whether good or bad, seldom go competely unnoticed by others, although we may think that they are in a sealed book.

Not only does the all-seeing eye of God detect our every word and action, but our innermost thoughts are also completely known to Him.

Be always aware that you are in the loving presence of your Father and you will more easily do good and avoid evil.

Before (God) no creature is hidden, but all are open and laid bare to the eyes of Him with whom we have to do. (Heb. 4:13)

Thanks to You, Lord, for Your ever faithful care for us.

Child's Message Inspires Millions

The post office could not deliver a Christmas greeting sent by nine-year-old Susan Long of Belleville, N.J.

It was addressed to "The Baby Jesus, Bethlehem" and read "Dear Jesus: I am writing to you instead of Santa because You are what Christmas is. I would like to say before we all forget, 'Happy Birthday,' and thank You for the present of You."

Even though the post office sent Susan's letter back with the notation "Returned for better address," her message reached people in many lands.

Within a few days newspapers all over the world had published her message. She received hundreds of letters praising her true Christmas spirit. The mayor of Bethlehem even airmailed Susan a Christmas gift.

No good effort, however insignificant it may seem, is ever in vain. In one way or another, God sees that the smallest prayer, word, or deed has an effect. We may never know the good accomplished but God sees and that counts above all else.

(Your) glory above the heavens is chanted by the mouth of babes and infants. (Ps. 8:2)

Keep me ever conscious, Holy Spirit, of the big blessing often hidden in little deeds.

Thanks to One Woman

One woman's determination, more than 100 years ago, was largely responsible for our present custom of a national Thanksgiving Day.

For 17 years Sarah Hale carried on a single-handed campaign through talks, letters, and magazine articles. She stressed how the nation would benefit if our gratitude to God was officially acknowledged on a specific day throughout the country instead of at a variety of times in various states.

Abraham Lincoln was impressed by Sarah Hale's impact on the nation. In his proclamation in 1863, setting the last Thursday of November as a national Day of Thanksgiving, Lincoln said:

"It has seemed to me fit and proper that God's blessings should be solemnly, reverently, and gratefully acknowledged, as with one heart and one voice, by the whole American people."

You, too, can do something to keep all aware that we owe much to God, the author of our liberty.

What shall I render to the Lord for all His bounty to me? (Ps. 116:12)

Thanks to You, bountiful Creator, for Your unending blessings on all of us.

How to Write an Effective Letter

You can help shape public opinion if you take the trouble to write constructive letters to those in positions of influence. Here are a few tips:

■ Be objective. Stick to the truth and back up your opinions with facts. Exaggerations, emotional outbursts, or extremes of any kind detract from your point and often cause a letter to be dropped unread into the waste basket.

■ Think things through. Instead of dashing off a few meaningless lines, take a few moments to clarify and coordinate your thoughts. This practice will add punch to your words.

■ Write promptly; don't delay. A brief note of praise or constructive criticism dispatched without delay makes a far greater impact than one sent when an issue is practically forgotten. Furthermore, postponement often means "never sent."

God wants you to show a personal responsibility towards the world in which you live. Letter writing can help you exert an influence for good.

By your words you will be justified, and by your words you will be condemned. (Mt. 12:37)

Allow me, Almighty God, to be an instrument in bringing Your love and truth to everyone.

Fire Travels Across Country

A railroad box car, carrying 53 bales of cotton once brought a fire from East to West.

The fire started in Lancaster, S.C., but was not discovered until the car reached Portland, Ore.

Firemen, finding the seals on the doors of the freight car unbroken, concluded that the fire had been smoldering for some time until it burned its way through a two-inch wooden flooring and then burst into flames.

A tiny spark probably started this fire. In much the same way, the little things we say or do may have repercussions, good or bad, in some distant place or even long after we have passed from the earthly scene.

This can be a most stimulating thought for those intent on doing as much good as possible during their pilgrimage through life.

If you truly desire to share your blessings with the world, as far as you can reach, God will bless you. One day when you stand before Him, you may be happily surprised to learn the far-reaching effects of your efforts.

"Yes, Lord; you know that I love You." He said to him, "Feed My lambs." (Jn. 21:15)

Imbue me with a consuming desire, Lord, to reach all humankind with Your divine love.

Ideas Are Needed

ew of us know how to express ourselves adequate-
because of this, we fail to spread the good ideas
d to us by God.

se of such neglect, the positions of influence of-
y default into the hands of those who are deter-
mislead rather than lead.

dvantage of every opportunity to communicate
ese few tips may help:

ember your importance as a connecting link be-
d and others. You may be the transmitter of divine
any a person who would never hear it except for

aint yourself with some fundamentals of public
ffective writing, and parliamentary procedure.
e all else, deepen your convictions — your love
l people. You will never stimulate others to ac-
ds come only from your lips, not from your

ak in the tongues of men and of angels, but
t love, I am a noisy gong or a clanging cymbal.
13:1)

o You, Holy Spirit, for the privilege of being a
or of Your divine truth.

They Walked Off With the Safe

One man who thought he had a burglar-proof safe got a rude awakening.

As an added protection, this careful individual had his new safe built into the wall of his New Jersey home. With this he felt fully confident that when he went out, his money, jewelry, and securities would be completely secure.

A couple of thieves, however, had a different point of view. After several vain attempts to open it, they agreed that the safe was a very good one. But they wouldn't let a seemingly impregnable safe stand in their way. They simply tore it out of the wall and took it with them.

There's nothing shy or backward about most evildoers. They could not be more persistent, painstaking, and thorough in seeing their objectives through to the finish.

Show as much zeal and stick-to-itiveness in championing the eternal truths of God and the human rights of everyone and you will do a service to one and all.

Who is there to harm you if you are zealous for what is right? (1 Pet. 3:13)

Grant, Lord, that I may be more steadfast in behalf of truth than anyone is for error.

One Man Stops 64 Trains

Sixty-four commuter trains, headed for New York during the morning rush hour not long ago were stopped by a hit-and-run driver.

One man delayed 45,000 individuals for as much as 35 minutes on their way to work.

All the trouble started when the motorist crashed into a pole supporting telephone and telegraph cables at the side of the tracks.

When the first pole toppled, the weight of the cables caused seven other poles to snap one by one.

The falling cables landed on the third rail, causing a short circuit. To prevent further trouble, railway officals cut off the power on all four tracks. One man thus compelled 45,000 others to sit and wait.

What one person does — or fails to do — can have far-reaching effects. The peace, happiness, and very destiny of countless individuals is involved in what we do. We will not know until we stand before the judgment seat of God how many people have been helped — or hurt — by what each of us thinks, says, and does.

The fruit of the righteous is a tree of life, but lawlessness takes away lives. (Prov. 11:30)

Let me be so busy serving the best interests of others, Jesus, that I will never risk harming them.

Lead More Than a Harml

A critic once summed up a mo
remarkable, but pleasant and no h

That terse judgment could also s
many people who contentedly live

It's easy to slip into a passive or
But those who smugly boast, "I'v
to anyone," and think that's the pe
miss the big reason for living.

Nowhere in the Gospels does O
it easy.

Jesus repeatedly stresses that
and not bury it by leading lives t
harmless.

He emphasizes that our very
positive good we do for other
trusted to us.

Do good, He commands.
Love your neighbor, He insist
just tolerating or refraining

**Maintain good conduc
. . . they may see your
on the day of visitati**

*Deepen in me, Lord,
deeds, not merely t*

Your

Too f
ly and,
entruste

Becau
ten go b
mined t

Take a
ideas. Th

■ Rem
tween Go
truth to m
you.

■ Acqu
speaking,

■ Abov
of God an
tion if wor
heart.

**If I sp
have no
(1 Cor.**

*Thanks
distribu*

Roots of Law

"The foundation of law is not opinion, but nature," said Cicero in 50 B.C.

In the 17th century Edward Coke, the distinguished English lawyer, reiterated this sublime thought.

"The law of nature is that which God at the time of creation of the nature of man infused into his heart for his preservation and direction; and this is the eternal law, the moral law, called also the law of nature."

It was on the cornerstone of natural law that the 56 Founding Fathers based the Declaration of Independence. They rooted their authority in the "laws of nature and nature's God."

They clearly stated that every individual has rights that no person or government can take away, rights that have their origin in the natural and consequently the eternal law.

Do your part to promote a respect for the natural law especially in these critical times when it is so often flaunted and catastrophe results.

Great peace have those who love Your law; nothing can make them stumble. (Ps. 119:165)

Thank you, Divine Lawgiver, for engraving on our hearts that truth which nothing can eradicate.

No Failure

Judged by ordinary standards, the life of Francis Thompson, the 19th century English poet, was a miserable failure. He failed successively as a student, a book agent, a shoemaker's apprentice, and a soldier.

At 21 he was a drug addict, prematurely aged, sleeping on park benches and writing poems on wrapping paper, making his living by running errands and selling matches.

Then he was discovered by an editor, Wilfrid Meynell, and his wife Alice, herself a poet. Thompson went to live with them, and stayed with them for years, until he died. He devoted himself wholeheartedly to his writings, and his talent was recognized.

Of his works, one, his great religious poem — "The Hound of Heaven" — won a place for itself among the most celebrated minor poems in our language.

Success is something we must find in our own way by cooperating with God. Poverty and hunger and neglect do not necessarily mean failure, though they are often mistaken for it. We fail only when we give ourselves up for lost, refusing the helping hand of others, persisting in despair.

The Lord will keep you from all evil; He will keep your life. The Lord will keep your going out and your coming in. (Ps. 121:8)

Grant, Lord, that I may see that life holds no failure like the failure to hope in You.

The Test of Friendship

True friendship is one of the greatest joys that human beings can experience. In a very real sense, it can be a foretaste of heaven.

Christ Himself said that the surest sign of sincere friendship is to lose oneself in order to gain for others. "Greater love than this no one has, that one lay down one's life for one's friend." (Jn. 15:13)

Real friends think more of giving than of receiving. They seek the good of others, regardless of the cost to themselves. Real friends gladly share sorrows as well as joys. They are as readily available in adversity as in success.

Real friends anticipate wants without ever intruding or imposing. They constantly look for ways to help the insecure feel both wanted and needed.

Because they first love others, they are usually beloved in return. By enriching other lives, they enrich their own.

True friendship is a gift of God, a foretaste of the joy of eternity, a beginning of heaven on earth.

A friend loves at all times. (Pr. 17:17)

Teach us to love others, Divine Redeemer, as You love us.

Launch Out Into the Deep

Many passages in the Gospels have special meaning for Christ-bearers. One in particular tells how Simon Peter was suddenly turned from a state of fearful caution in which he was accomplishing little to one of daring faith that brought about astonishing results.

"When (Jesus) had ceased speaking, He said to Simon, 'Put out into the deep and let down your nets for a catch.'

"And Simon answered, 'Master, we toiled all night and took nothing! But at Your word I will let down the nets.'

"And when they had done this, they enclosed a great shoal of fish; and as their nets were breaking, they beckoned to their partners in the other boat to come and help them. And they came and filled both the boats, so that they began to sink.

"But when Simon Peter saw it, he fell down at Jesus' knees, saying, 'Depart from me, for I am a sinful man, O Lord.' For he was astonished, and all that were with him, at the catch of fish which they had taken." (Lk. 5:4-9)

(Jesus) said to them, "Why are you afraid? Have you no faith?" (Mk. 4:40)

Lord, teach me to accept Your word readily, as Peter did.

'Should I Swear Falsely . . .'

A state supreme court justice once spoke about the oath witnesses take in court. Few people nowadays take it seriously, he complained.

He went on to show us an earlier oath, used by American courts in the last century. It goes:

"I do solemnly appeal to God, as a witness of the truth and the avenger of falsehood, and shall answer for the same at the great day of judgment, when the secrets of all hearts shall be known, that the evidence which I shall give in the case now on trial shall be the truth, the whole truth, and nothing but the truth, so help me God, upon penalty of the eternal damnation of my soul should I swear falsely."

If more witnesses today thought of their duties in the solemn light of this oath, surely justice would function more efficiently.

> **Do not speak evil against one another, brethren. He that speaks evil against a brother or judges (him) . . . speaks evil againt the law and judges the law . . . Who are you that you judge your neighbor? (Jas. 4:11-12)**

Lord, whose judgments are always just, teach me to seek justice in all my actions.

Good Medicine

Oliver Goldsmith is remembered as a great novelist and dramatist. But early in his life he was also a physician whose compassion for the sick and suffering went far beyond professional concern.

One day he was called to attend a very poor patient in Southwark, England. Sick as the patient was, the doctor saw that he had need of something more than medicine.

Taking all the money he had with him, Goldsmith put it into a large pill box and wrote on the label: "To be taken as occasion requires."

This act of thoughtfulness probably did more than anything else to hasten the recovery of the worried patient.

There are thousands of ways in which you can be considerate of others. Oftener than not, it takes only a moment and requires little sacrifice. It is one sure way to a start to restore peace to the world.

Whoever gives you a cup of water to drink because you bear the name of Christ, will by no means lose his reward. (Mk. 9:40)

Divine Physician, show me the many opportunities I have each day to bring Your compassion to others.

In Reverse

A successful businessman who could have brought much happiness into others' lives as well as his own made a revealing reply one day to a friend who had been trying to help him show more concern for the common good and less for his own selfish interests.

"I can't figure out what you mean," the businessman said. "I am interested in others. I do everything I can to make everybody like me."

Little did he realize how completely he had missed the point. He was frankly admitting that his only aim was to make everybody "like him." He was unaware that it was his Christian duty first to "like others."

The devil finds it easy to tempt us to the effort of attracting attention rather than giving attention to others. Pray that you will never succumb to this ruse of taking yourself too seriously and others not seriously enough.

In proportion as you love others "as you love yourself," so will you be happy here and hereafter.

> **Love is patient and kind; love is not jealous or boastful; it is not arrogant or rude. Love does not insist on its own way; it is not irritable or resentful; it does not rejoice at wrong but rejoices in the right. (1 Cor. 13:4-6)**

Lord, show me how to love others, whether or not they love me.

The First Vote

Paul Antonio, a tinsmith, was hired to build and install the black steel ballot box used by members of the United Nations Security Council at Lake Success when they first cast their votes on world issues.

When the box was opened just before the first Security Council session, there was at the bottom a brief message written in a clear handwriting on a cheap piece of notepaper. The message read:

"May I, who have had the privilege of constructing this ballot box, cast the first vote? May God be with every member of the United Nations Organization, and through your noble efforts bring lasting peace to us all — all over the world."

(Signed) Paul Antonio, mechanic

By this one simple act did Antonio (a workman, like Joseph, the foster father of Jesus) give the council members a reminder of the importance of the supernatural.

At the same time (because the incident was widely publicized for its human-interest angle) he got the same lesson over to millions in our land and throughout the world.

Peace I leave with you; My peace I give to you; not as the world gives do I give to you. (Jn. 14:27)

May I be alert, Jesus, to every opportunity to bring the true message of peace to others.

Follow the Signs

When Britain was in danger of invasion early in World War II, the people were told to destroy all signposts and direction indicators in the countryside in order to confuse enemy paratroopers, should they land.

In 1944, as soon as the danger had passed, the signs were immediately restored, since they were really vital to the successful life of the country.

Just as we cannot travel about the country without signs, so we cannot make our journey through life without some laws to tell us the right direction to follow.

A disordered life is like a journey that has no destination. Fortunately, God has given us clear signs: the natural law, the commandments, and above all the teachings of Christ.

These markers make the route clear to all of us; we have only to follow them.

I am the way, and the truth, and the life; no one comes to the Father, but by Me. (Jn. 14:6)

Jesus, help me keep the sight of Your cross always in mind so that I can be sure I am headed in the right direction to eternal life.

Worth Repeating

Dante, the great-hearted, large-minded example of all that was bright and good in medieval Christendom, once described the purpose of his writing in these beautiful words:

". . . I am the man who, when Love lectures in the heart, takes notes, and then retells the lessons to the rest of men."

Whether we are writers, teachers, government employees, trade unionists, businessmen or wage-earners, homemakers or students at school, we can — each one of us — reflect in our own relationships with others some small portion of the purpose and depth of understanding of the divine which made Dante the man he was.

We can listen to the lessons which the God who is Love teaches us through religion and prayer, through friends, through nature, through books, and make it our most joyous aim in life to bring that lesson to others.

Ask the beasts, and they will teach you; the birds of the air, and they will tell you; or the plants of the earth, and they will teach you; and the fish of the sea will declare to you. Who among all these does not know that the hand of the Lord has done this? (Job 13:7-9)

Lord, teach me Your lesson of love and enable me to retell it to others.

What's in a Book?

A friend of ours was complaining to his doctor that he "couldn't understand people."

Shaking his head, he added, "I've read all sorts of books on psychology, studied mental hygiene, taken a couple of years of 'psych' in college. I can't understand it; people simply puzzle me."

The doctor answered at once, "You're wasting your time trying to learn about human nature by reading books. You'll never understand people that way.

"You've got to live with people, work with them, mix with them. Books aren't the whole story. I find them useful chiefly as a guide to diagnosis."

Some people make the mistake of trying to learn about God merely by reading books about Him. To understand Him, you've got to live with Him, work with Him, talk with Him. We do this in prayer. But we must not neglect to look for Him as He is reflected in our fellow human beings.

(God) is not far from each one of us for "In Him we live and move and have our being." (Acts 17:28)

God, teach me to know You better by learning to love Your image in all others.

No Greater Gift

A Sunday school teacher was giving a talk on sacrifice to a fidgety group of youngsters. An unusual silence came over them. Their faces were wide-eyed with understanding. She emphasized that a real sacrifice to Christ was the gift of something dear to one's heart.

Late that afternoon, when the church was deserted and dim, a small figure crept up to the altar rail and hurriedly laid down a bundle. It was a dirty, torn, but beloved rag doll — Nancy's most precious gift to Christ.

What is important to God is not the gift but why and how it is given.

The gift God loves best from anyone is the gift of self. It is a real test of love, for it means a repeated and continued giving of self day by day — even hour by hour.

In the face of disappointments, ingratitude, loneliness, lack of cooperation, apathy and indifference, you will be buoyed up and spurred on because you realize that God Himself knows you are giving your all for love of Him.

Whatever gain I had, I counted as loss for the sake of Christ. Indeed I count everything as loss because of the surpassing worth of knowing Christ Jesus my Lord. (Phil. 3:7-8)

Holy Spirit, enlighten and strengthen me so that I may persevere in always preferring Christ Jesus to everyone and everything.

How You Say It Is Also Important

Aristotle, the renowned Greek philosopher, once said: "It is not enough to know what to say; it is necessary to know how to say it."

Many people with good ideas are flat failures at self expression. As a consequence they often bottle up the sound principles they know they should bring into public and private life.

You owe it to God, to yourself, and to your fellow human beings to acquire at least the elementary skills of how to say it if you are to be an effective force for good in these challenging times.

Do more than answer the roll call and then remain speechless at church, civic, school, union, political, fraternal, business or social meetings.

You have opportunities that no other person in the world can take advantage of. Live up to your responsibilities and help prevent leadership from slipping by default into the hands of the indifferent, incompetent or unprincipled.

Make it a point to be skilled in how to say it, as well as what to say.

Let your speech always be gracious, seasoned with salt, so that you may know how you ought to answer every one. (Col. 4:6)

Teach me, God, how to become a more alert and effective communicator of Your truth.

Fling Away Ambition

Wolsey was Henry VIII's teacher in statecraft, the man who had made England a power to be reckoned with. But when there was no longer any need for him, the unscrupulous king did not hesitate to get rid of his former adviser.

In Shakespeare's play, *Henry VIII*, the aging and worldly cardinal gives this advice to a young courtier:

I charge thee, fling away ambition:
By that sin fell the angels, . . .
Love thyself last: cherish those hearts that hate thee; . . .
Had I but served my God with half the zeal
I served my king, He would not in mine age
Have left me naked to mine enemies . . .

Self-reliance is a virtue that many justly admire, but to be really effective it must be rooted in faith in God. There is nothing wrong with ambition, if our desire is not a merely selfish one for worldly glory, but has always our eternal destiny in mind.

Seek first (your Father's) kingdom and His righteousness. (Mt. 6:33)

May our chief ambition always be to help bring God to others and others to God.

Reaching Everybody

A few summers ago I was in a group which went from Paris to the little town of Lisieux. Much of it was destroyed by the war, but not the convent where a French woman had entered at age 15 and died at 24: Therese of Lisieux, the Little Flower of Jesus.

She, probably more than anyone else who has lived in our day, has reached millions simply by loving everybody the world over. In some mystic way they came to know of her, to feel sure that she cared for each of them individually.

Her whole secret is expressed in her own words inscribed above her tomb: "I would like to spend my heaven doing good on earth."

She understood the important difference between merely "being" good and "doing" good; between being just a "hearer" and not a "doer." And because she wanted to reach others with her love, the Lord blessed her.

Once you start "doing" good, you deepen, strengthen, and increase your "being" good. You, too, will start to reach out in love to all as far as you can. It may well be, then, that God will bless you as He has blessed Therese.

Be doers of the word, and not hearers only, deceiving yourselves. For if any one is a hearer of the word and . . . a doer that acts, he shall be blessed. (Jas. 1:22-23,25)

Lord, help me to spend my life bringing You to as many as I can.

How to Be Attractive

A community in Pennsylvania announced a charm school designed to make teachers more attractive. The printed sales talk went like this:

"Would you like to know some of the hair-dos becoming to different types?

"Does your voice have that quality which makes pupils want to listen?"

No doubt there is certain merit in a charm school. Most of us could stand a bit of it.

But the real charm that most need is the charm that comes from developing the mind, heart and soul in the ways of Christ.

You can do this by being gentle instead of abrupt, by giving attention instead of only seeking it, by adapting yourself to others instead of expecting them always to fit into your plans, by praising and not blaming, by encouraging in place of discouraging.

> **The Lord sees not as man sees; man looks on the outward appearance, but the Lord looks on the heart. (1 Sam. 16:7)**

> *Teach me, Lord, to develop in myself that inner charm that must precede any exterior charm.*

Share Your Good News

Several years ago an elderly doctor in New England discovered a remarkably effective cure for asthma which proved to be successful in eight out of every ten cases.

"Why, that's wonderful!" a friend congratulated him as soon as he heard of it. And then he suggested: "But you ought to put it on the market so it can reach more people."

The suggestion fell on deaf ears. The doctor, preoccupied with his own small group of patients, neglected to take any measures to make his discovery available to millions. A short time later the doctor died and his cure, of course, died with him.

Limited vision and possessiveness on our part deprive countless others of blessings that God meant for them — and meant to get to them through us!

Do not reject an afflicted suppliant, nor turn your face away from the poor. Do not avert your eye from the needy, nor give a man occasion to curse you. (Sir. 4:4-5)

May I never withhold whatever means and talents I have for helping others, Jesus.

A Man of Vision

"There is one task that only a world community can achieve — the never-ending and collective task of turning, first, into clear ideas all that human heads can think, and then into concrete things all that human hands can make."

These are not the words of a statesman of the 20th century. They were written more than 650 years ago by a man who has been loved and admired by millions for his world vision, his wisdom, his compassion. His name was Dante Alighieri, patriot and poet, soldier and statesman.

Anyone who grasps even a fraction of such broad vision and who strives to communicate it to others can be a channel of grace, an instrument of the peace and truth of Christ. For even Dante's world vision was but a reflection of the world vision of Our Lord.

It is only because we are made in the image of God that we can reflect that vision of His at all. And each time we strive to bring some glimpse of it to others, we glorify Him in Whose image we are made.

> **Male and female He created them. And God blessed them, and God said to them, "Be fruitful and multiply, and fill the earth and subdue it . . ." (Gen. 1:27-28)**

> *Creator, in whose image we are made, grant that we may reflect in our daily lives Your world vision.*

Do You Have True Compassion?

"By compassion we make another's misery our own." This is an excellent definition of the word compassion, which originates from the two Latin terms: "cum" meaning "with" and "patior" meaning "to suffer."

When you have true compassion for another who is in trouble, show it by more than an empty expression. You indicate that you are willing to suffer with another individual and even make considerable personal sacrifice to relieve his distress.

Vast numbers of people over the earth have been waiting, almost in vain, for enough individuals with true compassion in their hearts to help them solve their staggering problems of hunger, homelessness, poverty, lack of water, weak governments, inadequate education, labor unrest, and economic instability.

Christ Himself gave us the example to imitate. At all times He had compassion on the multitude. He made the misery of others His own concern.

> **(Jesus) saw a great throng, and He had compassion on them because they were like sheep without a shepherd. (Mk. 6:34)**

> *Jesus, help me to make the cause of the poor and afflicted my own cause.*

Recipe for Happiness

Those who are bored with life should try this recipe for happiness, penned by an unknown author:

"Do all the good you can,

"In all the ways you can,

"To all the people you can."

It is a human tendency to shy away from the time and effort involved in personally helping others. As a result many people go through an entire lifetime without realizing how much they cheat themselves by the selfish formula: "Take out of life as much as you can and put in as little as possible."

Look for every opportunity to open your heart to the full capacity intended by your Creator. He has given you a heart big enough to embrace the whole world.

Always remember that your pilgrimage through life is brief at best. Imitate Christ in seeking every opportunity to "do all the good you can to all the people you can."

You will have a foretaste of the endless joy of paradise if you do.

> **Owe no one anything, except to love one another; for he who loves his neighbor has fulfilled the law. The Commandments . . . are summed up in this sentence, "You shall love your neighbor as yourself." (Rom. 13:8-9)**

Lord and lover of souls, let me do as much good as I can for as many as I can.

The Power of the Writer

Emerson once said: "Talent alone cannot make a writer. There must be a man behind the book."

Words convey thoughts that are good, bad, or indifferent depending on whether the individual who writes them is constructive, destructive, or neutral.

In today's world, one writer may shape the thought of hundreds, thousands, even millions. Behind every newspaper article or book, there is frequently just one individual.

The songs that millions sing, the textbooks that shape the minds of innumerable students, the publications that trade unionists and businessmen read are all written by individuals.

How important then that every writer be endowed with high ideals and a sense of responsibility as well as the necessary competence.

You can render a service to God and your fellow human beings by encouraging some talented young person to dedicate his or her life to a writing career.

The word of God is living and active, sharper than any two-edged sword, piercing to the division of soul and spirit, of joints and marrow, and discerning the thoughts and intentions of the heart. (Heb. 4:12)

Inspire more who are talented and conscientious to become writers, Jesus.

Success in Failure

For centuries no one knew who had been the architect for one of the most beautiful and most durable of ancient monuments — the Coliseum.

Then one day, during the 17th century, excavators, digging among the ruins of Rome, came upon a marble slab. The slab uncovered the secret of the centuries.

Carved on it were the crown and palm — symbols of martyrdom. The inscription praised a man named Gaudentius, mentioning that he was the architect of the Coliseum, and ironically enough, one of its first martyrs. It reads:

"Caesar had promised three great rewards, but false and ungrateful was the pagan; He who is the great architect of the heavens and Whose promises fail not, has prepared for thee in reward of thy virtue a place in the everlasting theater of the celestial city."

In the eyes of the world the once successful Gaudentius had become a failure. But not in the sight of God. He fulfilled his one big purpose in life — to live and die for God. What greater success could a man have?

There is no one who has left house or brothers or sisters or mother or father or children or lands, for My sake and for the gospel, who will not receive a hundredfold now in this time . . . with persecutions, and in the age to come eternal life. (Mk. 10:29-30)

God, help me to place my hopes for success in You alone.

Back to the Classroom

A 58-year-old Connecticut woman proved how parents of grown families can effectively serve their communities.

Before her marriage, she had taught school for 13 years. When her children were grown and able to take care of themselves, she felt that it was important to continue as a creative contributor.

She not only returned to the classroom, but worked for a degree on the side so she could be a better teacher.

She summed up her motivation in these few words: "It's wonderful to work with living souls."

Those who are in love with people for love of God, are never content to sit on the sidelines as mere spectators of life.

Some, in their relentless but mistaken search for happiness, seek to take as much as they can out of life. However, those who know true values realize that lasting peace of mind and heart is only to be found by giving oneself for the sake of others.

They prove that "It's wonderful to work with living souls."

> **Whatever you do, in word or deed, do everything in the name of the Lord Jesus, giving thanks to God the Father through Him. (Col. 3:17)**

> *Enable me to grow in love for people, God, and thus grow in my love for You.*

Three Ways to Inspire Children

Here are three tips for parents:

■ Treat each child as an individual — God gives slightly different talents and personalities to every child He sends into the world.

Though it may take years to find the particular qualities buried in every boy and girl, the search is worth every effort.

■ Encourage their desire to contribute — Every child has a basic desire to be useful and constructive. Though this is part of his God-given nature, a youngster's better impulses are often offset by human weaknesses. Each one, therefore, needs unending encouragement and sympathetic guidance to lead a worthwhile life.

■ Help them to think and act for themselves — The creative side of children is almost limitless. Avoid the danger of nipping in the bud a young person's natural instinct to be reasonably self-reliant.

Too much independence too soon, of course, can hurt children. But it is even more damaging to regiment their every move.

Train up a child in the way he should go, and when he is old he will not depart from it. (Prov. 22:6)

Keep us mindful, Lord, that You have given a distinct individuality to every child.

He Showed Hollywood

A five-year-old refugee was being shown around a Hollywood department store by his American foster parents. When they came to the toy department, crowded with playthings in preparation for the Christmas rush, the little boy's eyes grew wide with wonderment.

He examined the many items with amazed delight, but gradually the grownups noticed an expression of disappointment clouding the boy's face. He began to search up and down aisles, under tables, and behind counters.

At last, when questioned what he was looking for, he burst out: "But where is the Child?"

There was an embarrassed silence. Then a store official gave instructions for a Christmas crib to be found at once and set up in a prominent place in the toy department. And at this the little boy smiled with delight.

Young as he was, he had given a lesson in the real significance of Christmas. He had pointed out the grave oversight of overlooking the One for whom the birthday party was being given!

To us a Child is born, to us a Son is given . . . and His name will be called "Wonderful Counselor, Mighty God, Everlasting Father, Prince of Peace." (Is. 9:6)

Pray that you may carry the spirit of Christmas in your heart all through the coming year.

That I May See!

Blind since birth, nine-year-old Sylvia Ayale of Puerto Rico underwent an operation for the removal of cataracts from both eyes.

When the bandages were removed just before Christmas, Sylvia was able to see for the first time in her life.

At a Christmas party shortly after the operation, she was given a pretty white dress with red trimmings and a big doll. With great joy and gratitude she repeated over and over again, "I can see! I can see! Merry Christmas!"

Few have any idea what it means to be born blind — to be deprived of the blessing of sight.

Likewise, it's difficult for the well-fed to appreciate hunger, for the healthy to understand the sick, for those who enjoy economic and political security to sympathize with those who know only insecurity, for those who possess the blessings of faith to appreciate the compassionate kindness of their God.

God, in the person of Jesus, chose to be born as a human being. God thus knows what it is like to be human.

(Jesus) had to be made like His brethren in every respect, so that He might become a merciful and faithful high priest in the service of God. . . . because He Himself has suffered and been tempted, He is able to help those who are tempted. (Heb. 2:17-18)

Jesus, enable me to empathize with others as You empathize with me.

More Than Words Needed

Visitors to the Cathedral in Lubeck, Germany, are usually impressed by an old inscription that reads:

Thus speaketh Christ our Lord to us:
You call me Master, and obey me not;
You call me Light, and see me not;
You call me Way, and walk me not;
You call me Life, and desire me not;
You call me Wise, and follow me not;
You call me Fair, and love me not;
You call me Rich, and ask me not;
You call me Eternal, and seek me not;
You call me Gracious, and trust me not;
You call me Noble, and serve me not;
You call me Mighty, and honor me not;
You call me Just, and fear me not;
If I condemn you, blame me not.

More than lip service is needed to prove our love for God or our fellow human beings. Back up noble words with practical deeds and you will make a personal contribution to the peace of the world.

Not every one who says to me, "Lord, Lord," shall enter the kingdom of heaven, but he who does the will of My Father who is in heaven. (Mt. 7:21)

Infant Savior, show me how to put the Will of the Father into effect in my life.

Do More Than Find Fault

"It is better to light one candle than curse the darkness."

This is the motto of The Christophers. It reminds us all that the smallest constructive word or deed is far more valuable than any amount of fault-finding.

It is easy to slip into the habit of complaining and criticizing. But little if anything comes from such a negative approach.

Instead of sitting on the sidelines bemoaning evil trends and waiting for the world to fall in on top of you, do your part to meet the crucial problems of our day.

The smallest effort to right what is wrong in home life, politics, education, labor unions, or any other sphere of influence is at least one step in the right direction.

Stand up to trouble, confront it, overcome it and everybody will be indebted to you.

Overcome evil with good. (Rom. 12:21)

Let me be a doer rather than a complainer, Lord.

Taught to Steal

Few parents teach their children to steal. But one 14-year-old boy in San Diego, who was caught taking an electric tool in a downtown store, told the police how his parents showed him how to steal.

He described the year of training they gave him. It included shoplifting, picking pockets, and auto thefts. The police doubted his story until they checked the dates and places he mentioned.

To avoid prosecution, his parents disappeared immediately after the boy's arrest, taking the family trailer with them. Warrants charged the couple with burglary, receiving stolen property, and contributing to the delinquency of a minor.

While there is little danger of many parents leading their children into a life of crime, they can easily neglect the thorough training that will put youngsters on the road to heaven. Children need guidance and inspiration to live worthwhile lives.

Whoever causes one of these little ones who believe in Me to sin, it would be better for him to have a great millstone fastened round his neck and to be drowned in the depth of the sea. (Mt. 18:6)

Father, remind all parents of the privilege that is theirs in shaping young lives for time and eternity.

Driver Deserts Bus Passengers

December 28

A bus driver, upset by the way motorists drive, quit his job in the middle of an intercity run on Vancouver Island, B.C.

He wheeled his big bus with its 41 passengers to the side of the highway, picked up his jacket and cash box and then politely announced to the startled people: "That's it, I quit."

An hour and a half passed before a relief driver could complete the run.

In explaining his drastic action, the exasperated driver said: "I'm getting fed up with the way people drive. They just drive for the maximum inconvenience of everyone."

Those who are quite sensitive to inconsiderateness by others can be very blind to the unfair way in which they themselves may act.

In your home, at work, in school or anywhere else, follow the divine standard of treating others as you would like them to treat you. You will thus be taking a few steps to right the wrongs of the world.

As you wish that men would do to you, do so to them. (Lk. 6:31)

Let me show the same consideration for others, Jesus, that I expect from them.

The Price of Peace

Practically everybody in the world wants peace. But too many people overlook the fact that peace, which is the "tranquility of order," is never achieved by mere wishful thinking.

"Blessed are the peacemakers," said the Prince of Peace. He did not say blessed are those who only sit and talk about peace without ever taking the difficult steps to bring it about.

To be a peacemaker or a maker of peace usually means inconvenience and hard work.

Heartaches and heartbreaks are the customary price you must pay to apply divine love to your home, organization, community, state, country, or world.

Remember that the peace of the world starts with you as much as it does with anyone. If you realize this, you will equip yourself to play a decisive role in shaping the peace which God wishes all humankind to enjoy on earth.

Wisdom from above is first pure, then peaceable, gentle, open to reason, full of mercy and good fruits, without uncertainty or insincerity. And the harvest of righteousness is sown in peace by those who make peace. (Jas. 3:17-18)

Prince of Peace, teach me to be a peacemaker rather than just talk about peace.

Greed Is a Strange Master

December 30

A 28-year shopping spree came to an abrupt end when a 49-year-old woman was convicted of stealing a $2 pair of gloves.

While investigating the case, police found her modest six-room flat in Watford, England, crammed to the ceiling with some 60,000 pieces of merchandise. The wide assortment of items accumulated over nearly three decades was piled so high that it was necessary for the woman and her daughter to make "tunnels" to get from one section of the house to another.

Police said there was no evidence that the strange collection of merchandise had been stolen.

Excessive or inordinate desire for gain afflicts many of us. We pay a high price for our greed.

Strive, in Christ's Name, to share your material advantage with the poor and you will not run the risk of becoming a slave to the good things of earth.

He who loves money will not be satisfied with money; nor he who loves wealth, with gain. (Ec. 5:10)

Show me, God, how to value and use the good things of earth without becoming their slave.

Find Purpose in Your Work

Without so much as a blush, a meter reader in England admitted that he had never read a water meter in the last seven years.

"Some were in pig-sties," he said, "others in haystacks. One was even in a field with a big bull. Many meant a dirty job of digging down to them. They were not like light and gas meters — easy to get at."

After giving up on the effort, he resorted to sheer guess work, relying on water bills from previous years.

"I liked everything about the job," he admitted, "except reading those meters. They became a bore."

Nobody likes dirty jobs. But, like it or not, they have to be done.

Stop to think every so often about why God put you into his world. By directing your activities in the light of eternity, you will be more likely to be so busy helping other people that you won't have time to be bored. The stakes are so high in this nuclear age that none of us can afford to be mediocre.

The Lord recompense you for what you have done, and a full reward be given you by the Lord, the God of Israel. (Ruth 2:12)

Let me view my work, Lord, as another opportunity to share in Your creation and to serve my fellow human beings.

Also Available
From The Christophers

If you have enjoyed this book and are not familiar with our other offerings, here is a brief description of material available to the public.

■ News Notes. Some 30 titles are kept in stock. Any title can be obtained in quantities of 100 or more. Single copies of back issues, and all future issues, are free on request. Ask for our fulfillment brochure for information on back issues.

■ Ecos Cristoforos. Spanish translations of the most popular issues of News Notes. These too can be obtained in quantity. Single copies are free on request. A fulfillment brochure is available.

■ Appointment Calendar. The calendar is large enough to hang on the wall or keep handy on a desk. It contains an inspirational message for each day of the year and a generous amount of space for daily reminders, appointments, birthdays, etc.

■ Videocassettes. There are now more than 60 titles in our Videocassette Library. They range from wholesome entertainment to serious discussion to religious instruction. Family life, substance abuse, contemporary social issues, health concerns and spiritual growth are some of the topics available. Write for a free brochure.

Address all mail to:
THE CHRISTOPHERS, 12 East 48th St., New York, NY 10017